BEST
POEMS

Middle Level

Poems for Young People

with Lessons for Teaching the Basic Elements of Literature

JAMESTOWN PUBLISHERS

a division of NTC/CONTEMPORARY PUBLISHING GROUP
Lincolnwood, Illinois USA

Editorial Development: Patricia Opaskar, Mary Ann Trost
Cover Design: Steve Straus
Cover Illustration: Lori Lohstoeter
Interior Design: Steve Straus
Interior Illustrations: Pat Doyle

ISBN: 0-89061-892-5 (hardbound)
ISBN: 0-89061-848-8 (softbound)

Published by Jamestown Publishers,
a division of NTC/Contemporary Publishing Group, Inc.,
4255 West Touhy Avenue,
Lincolnwood (Chicago), Illinois 60712-1975 U.S.A.
© 1998 by NTC/Contemporary Publishing Group, Inc.

7 8 9 10 11 12 13 14 044 / 055 08 07 06 05

ACKNOWLEDGMENTS

Acknowledgment is gratefully made to the following publishers, authors, and agents for permission to reprint these works. Every effort has been made to determine copyright owners. In the case of any omissions, the Publisher will be pleased to make suitable acknowledgments in future editions.

Anderson, Jack. "Where You Are" from *The Invention of New Jersey* by Jack Anderson, © 1969. Reprinted by permission of the University of Pittsburgh Press.

Basho. "An old silent pond" from *Cricket Songs: Japanese Haiku* translated by Harry Behn. © 1964 Harry Behn. Copyright © renewed 1992 by Prescott Behn, Pamela Behn Adam and Peter Behn. Reprinted by permission of Marian Reiner.

Basho, Matsuo. "Clouds now and then" (p 112, 24 lines) by Matsuo Basho in *The Penguin Book of Japanese Verse* translated by Geoffrey Bownas and Anthony Thwaite (Penguin Books, 1964) copyright © Geoffrey Bownas and Anthony Thwaite, 1964. Reproduced by Penguin Books Ltd.

Blaine, Scott. "Hockey" from *Grab Me A Bus . . . And Other Award Winning Poems* by Malcolm Glass and M. Joe Eaton. Copyright © 1971 by Scholastic Inc. Reprinted by permission of Scholastic Inc.

Clifton, Lucille. "the mississippi river empties into the gulf," copyright © 1996 by Lucille Clifton. Reprinted from *The Terrible Stories* with the permission of BOA Editions, Ltd., 260 East Ave., Rochester, NY 14604.

Coatsworth, Elizabeth. "On a Night of Snow" from *Night and the Cat* by Elizabeth Coatsworth. Copyright 1950 The Macmillan Company. Reprinted by permission of Kate Barnes.

de la Mare, Walter. "The Listeners" from *The Complete Poems of Walter de la Mare*, 1969. Reprinted by permission of The Literary Trustees of Walter de la Mare and the Society of Authors as their representative.

Deutsch, Babette. "Fireworks" from *Collected Poems: 1919-1962* by Babette Deutsch. Published by Indiana University Press: First appeared in *The New Yorker*, October 20, 1962. Reprinted by permission of Adam Yarmolinsky, Executor of The Estate of Babette Deutsch.

Dickinson, Emily. "I'm nobody who are you" and "Bee! I'm expecting you!" are reprinted by permission of the publishers and the Trustees of Amherst College from *The Poems of Emily Dickinson*, Thomas H. Johnson, ed., Cambridge, Mass.: The Belknap Press of Harvard University Press, Copyright © 1951, 1955, 1979, 1983 by the President and Fellows of Harvard College.

Frost, Robert. "The Runaway," "Nothing Gold Can Stay," and "A Time to Talk" from *The Poetry of Robert Frost*, edited by Edward Connery Lathem, Copyright 1944, 1951 by Robert Frost, Copyright 1916, 1923, © 1969 by Henry Holt and Company, Inc., © 1997 Edward Connery Lathem. Reprinted by permission of Henry Holt and Company, Inc.

Hayden, Robert. "Those Winter Sundays", copyright © 1966 by Robert Hayden, from *Angle of Ascent: New and Selected Poems* by Robert Hayden. Reprinted by permission of Liveright Publishing Corporation.

Hunt, Evelyn Tooley. "Mama Is a Sunrise" from *The Lyric*, 1972. Reprinted by permission of Donald E. Hunt.

Kell, Richard. "Pigeons" from *Differences* by Richard Kell. Reprinted by permission of Chatto & Windus.

Kooser, Ted. "First Snow" is reprinted from *Sure Signs: New And Selected Poems* by Ted Kooser, by permission of the University of Pittsburgh Press. © 1980 by Ted Kooser.

Levertov, Denise. "Living" from *Poems 1960-1967*. Copyright © 1966 by Denise Levertov. Reprinted by permission of New Directions Publishing Corp.

Lutz, Gertrude May. "African Sunrise" from *Contemporary Poetry* (Winter 1944).

Marquis, Don. "The Lesson of the Moth" from *Archy and Mehitabel* by Don Marquis. Copyright 1927 by Doubleday, a division of Bantam, Doubleday, Dell Publishing Group, Inc. Used by permission of Doubleday, a division of Bantam Doubleday Dell Pubishing Group, Inc.

McGahey, Jeanne. "Oregon Winter," reprinted by permission of John Hart.

Mora, Pat. "Legal Alien" and "Petals" are reprinted with permission from the publisher of *Chants* (Houston: Arte Publico Press—University of Houston, 1985.)

Morris, John N. "Running it Backward" is reprinted with the permission of Scribner, a Division of Simon & Schuster from *The Life Beside This One* by John N. Morris. Copyright © 1975 John N. Morris. (First appeared in the Hudson Review).

Morrison, Lillian. "The Sprinters" from *The Sidewalk Racer and Other Poems of Sports and Motion* by Lillian Morrison. Copyright © 1965, 1967, 1968, 1977 by Lillian Morrison. © Renewed Lillian Morrison. Reprinted by permission of Marian Reiner for the author.

Oliver, Mary. "Sleeping in the Forest" from *Twelve Moons* by Mary Oliver. Copyright 1978 by Mary Oliver. First appeared in *Ohio Review*. Reprinted by permission of Little, Brown & Company.

Parker, Dorothy. "One Perfect Rose," copyright 1926, renewed © 1954 by Dorothy Parker, from *The Portable Dorothy Parker*, Introduction by Brendan Gill. Used by permission of Viking Penguin, a division of Penguin Putnam, Inc.

Pastan, Linda. "whom do you visualize as your reader?" from *The Five Stages of Grief* by Linda Pastan. Copyright © 1978 by Linda Pastan. Reprinted by permission of W.W. Norton & Company, Inc.

Polanco, Julio Noboa. "Identity" by Julio Noboa Polanco. Reprinted by permission of Julio Noboa Polanco. Written by Julio Polanco as an 8th-grade student.

Ruffin, Paul. "Cleaning the Well" by Paul Ruffin, first appeared in *Lighting the Furnace Pilot* (Spoon River Poetry Press, 1980). Reprinted by permission of the author.

Salinas, Luis Omar. "My Father Is a Simple Man" by Luis Omar Salinas is reprinted with permission from the publisher of *The Sadness of Days: Selected and New Poems* (Houston: Arte Publico Press—University of Houston, 1987.)

Sandburg, Carl. "Grass" from *Cornhuskers* by Carl Sandburg, copyright 1918 by Holt, Rinehart and Winston and renewed 1946 by Carl Sandburg, reprinted by permission of Harcourt Brace & Company.

(continued on page 246)

CONTENTS

TO THE STUDENT

Whenever we sleep soundly, we dream. Our minds call up images from normal life in an abnormal order. We can find ourselves swimming through grocery stores or joining long-ago playmates at lunch at a house we no longer live in. By the time we wake up, the unreal images are usually gone and we consider them unimportant. Scientific experiments have revealed how wrong that attitude is, however. Volunteers for dream-research projects have been kept from dreaming. Observant researchers wake them up every time brain signals indicate that dreams are beginning. After a few dreamless nights, the volunteers lose their ability to deal with normal life. They can spend eight hours sleeping, but the sleep doesn't refresh them. They are always tired and are unable to think straight. The researchers have concluded that, for various reasons, we need to dream.

In a way, poems are like dreams. They call up images from normal life in interesting and unusual ways. Reading some poems in a strictly logical way leaves us with a feeling of confusion, just as remembering a dream may. Yet when we let ourselves react to the images, the music, the form, and the weird logic of poems, they take on meaning and importance. They take us a step back from normal life and let us see normal events in a new way. Experiencing poems can help us appreciate the pleasant things in reality with greater awareness and deal with the undesirable things with more creativity. Like dreams, poems refresh us and leave us more capable of coping with life.

In this book, you will read poems by more than 50 poets. They will share their distinctive views of life through the shapes, sounds, and meanings of their words and the images those words create in your mind. They will relate stories, tell of personal weaknesses and triumphs, and draw you into moments of excitement and contentment. You will have many opportunities to broaden your own outlook and adapt some of your ideas about life.

The lessons in this book will help you recognize how the writers constructed their poems. You will learn about the major elements of poetry and the techniques poets use. You also will have a chance to try these techniques in your own writing. Perhaps you will find, as these writers did, that in expressing your thoughts, feelings, and dreams to others, they will make more sense to you.

UNIT FORMAT AND ACTIVITIES

- Each unit begins with a list of all the poems you will read in that unit. About the Lessons explains why the poems are grouped the way they are. In general, poems are grouped together because they are particularly good examples of one element of poetry that will be taught in that unit.
- The unit's major writing exercise is then introduced. In this exercise you will begin planning for the writing project that you will complete at the end of the unit. Periodically through-out the unit, you will have opportunities to explore and develop ideas for your writing project.
- About This Poet focuses on one important poet whose work appears in that unit. Here you will learn about the poet's life, major accomplishments, and works.
- Next, there are questions for you to ask yourself as you read the poems in the unit.
- The poems themselves make up the next section. Before each poem is a short biography of the poet and/or further informa-tion about the poem. These notes have been included because knowing something about a poet and the poem's con-tent may help you better understand and appreciate the work.
- Following the poems are questions that test your comprehen-sion and critical thinking skills. Your answers to these ques-tions and to other exercises in the unit should be recorded in a personal literature notebook. You also should check your answers with your teacher.
- Your teacher may provide you with charts to record your progress in developing your comprehension skills: The

Comprehension Skills Graph *records* your scores and the Comprehension Skills Profile *analyzes* your scores—providing you with information about the skills on which you need to focus. You can talk with your teacher about ways to work on those comprehension skills.

- The next section contains two or three lessons, which begin with a discussion of the literary concept that is the unit's focus. Each lesson illustrates one or more techniques that poets use to develop the concept. For example, you will see how a poet uses sensory details and concrete language to create memorable images.
- Short-answer exercises test your understanding of the poets' techniques as illustrated in particular poems that appear in the unit. You can check your answers to the exercises with your teacher and determine what you need to review.
- Each lesson also includes a writing exercise that guides you in creating your own original work using the techniques you have just studied.
- Discussion guides and a final writing activity round out each unit in the book. These activities will help sharpen your reading, thinking, speaking, and writing skills.
- At the back of the book is a discussion of the writing process. You may want to refer to it as you complete your writing exercises and projects. You also will find a glossary of literary terms. You can refer to the glossary when you encounter an unfamiliar term or concept.

Reading the poems in this book will enable you to recognize and appreciate the skills it takes to write a good poem. When you understand what makes a poem good, you will be better able to choose and enjoy worthwhile poems on your own. The writing exercises will help you become a better writer by giving you practice in using other poets' techniques to make your own poetry more effective and appealing.

What Is a Poem?

INTRODUCTION

ABOUT THE LESSONS

What do you think of when you hear the term *poetry*? Pretty language? Someone talking about flowers or feelings? Rhyming words on a greeting card? Certainly poetry can be involved in these things, but the definition and uses of poetry extend much further.

Poetry also can tell of mythical heroes and modern mysteries. It can be a tool for fighting indifference and injustice. It can give people a voice and help them express their hopes, doubts, confusions, and fears. Sometimes its language is flowery but not always. Sometimes it rhymes but not always. It is difficult to find a single description that fits all poetry. However, one thing that is almost always true is that in poetry writers share powerful thoughts, feelings, and experiences through the use of striking and unusual language.

The lessons in this unit will discuss some of the qualities that are found in most poems. Group 1 contains examples of some interesting language used by poets. Group 2 contains poems in which poets use the sounds of words to express or emphasize their ideas. Group 3 contains poems that illustrate how poets share their views and experiences in intense and personal ways.

 WRITING: BECOMING AWARE OF POETRY

As you progress through this book, you will see that poets use a variety of techniques to write effective poetry. At the end of this unit you will write a poem of your own in which you use some of those techniques. Here are some ideas to help you get started:

- The building blocks of poetry are all around you. Start to listen for elements of poetry in your daily life. Begin by carrying around a notebook and recording interesting comparisons that you may hear. For example, you may hear someone say that students are "packed like sardines into a school bus." Also record words and phrases that describe sights, sounds, smells, tastes, or feelings in particularly unique ways.

- Listen for examples of interesting or surprising uses of sounds in what you read or hear. Good sources for sounds are advertisements, such as television commercials, jingles, and slogans. You also may hear memorable uses of sounds in everyday conversations. Record any sounds that appeal to you or capture your attention.
- Also record words and phrases that appeal to your emotions. For example, list words that make you feel sad or optimistic, or that fill you with energy or calm you down.

ABOUT THIS POET

Walt Whitman (1819–1892) was born in Long Island, New York, and moved to Brooklyn, New York, when he was four years old. At the age of 10, he was apprenticed to a printer and later worked at that trade in New York City before becoming a teacher back in Long Island. Eager to return to the excitement of New York City, Whitman then took jobs as a printer and a journalist in the New York City area. While working at his various jobs, he began writing poetry. In 1855, he published his first edition of *Leaves of Grass*. The form and content of his poems were so unusual that he could not find a publisher willing to publish his book, so he published it at his own expense. The volume was met with little enthusiasm by critics and the public.

At one point Whitman started his own newspaper, the *Freeman*, but was forced to close it down because of political pressure. During the Civil War, Whitman served as a volunteer in military hospitals in Washington, D.C., and after the war he worked at government jobs until he suffered a paralyzing stroke in 1873. At that time he relocated to Camden,

New Jersey, where he continued revising and adding to *Leaves of Grass* until he died in 1892.

Whitman thought of himself as the poet of democracy. In many of his poems he praises the United States and its form of government. He once wrote, "The United States themselves are essentially the greatest poem." Whitman turned his back on traditional rhythm patterns and wrote in a more natural, conversational, and modern style, using what has come to be called *free verse*. Among his better-known poems are "O Captain! My Captain!" and "When Lilacs Last in the Dooryard Bloom'd" (both of which mourn the loss of President Abraham Lincoln); "Song of Myself"; and "I Sing the Body Electric."

AS YOU READ

As you read each of the poems in this unit, ask yourself these questions:

- How do the words that the poet uses appeal to my senses?
- How do the sounds and/or the visual form of the poem help to get my attention? How do they help to express the poem's meaning?
- What idea or feeling is the poem about? Have I ever thought or felt this way?
- Does the poem contain comparisons that help me make connections that I was never aware of before? If so, how and why?

African Sunrise

by Gertrude May Lutz

ABOUT THE SELECTION

Gertrude May Lutz (1899–   ) was born in Oakland, California, and has lived most of her life there. Although she attended business college, her chosen career was to write and teach poetry. Lutz has published five volumes of poetry and has had many of her poems included in poetry anthologies. She also has received a number of state and national poetry prizes. Look for the surprising combinations of images that she has included in "African Sunrise."

Sky
Over the last star;
The parrot-winds
Sharp-beaked with yellow
Nipping the bunched date palms . . .

Now the camels
Open their beeswax eyes
And raise long necks,
Rutted[1] sound in their throats—
Camels, pock-marking the sand with spread knees,
Lifting the odor of under-body with them.

Sun—
The burn of it
Hot-coined to each eyelid,
And desert-stretched,
        the caravan of hours
            not yet begun.

---

[1]as if going over tracks or grooves

Pigeons

by Richard Kell

ABOUT THE SELECTION

Richard Kell (1927–) was born in Ireland and graduated from Trinity College at the University of Dublin. He has been a college teacher, librarian, and lecturer and has written poems, essays, and short stories for a number of anthologies. In this poem look for the striking descriptions of a type of bird that is not universally loved.

They paddle with staccato[1] feet
in powder-pools of sunlight,
small blue busybodies
strutting like fat gentlemen
with hands clasped
under their swallowtail[2] coats;
and, as they stump about,
their heads like tiny hammers
tap at imaginary nails
in non-existent walls.
Elusive ghosts of sunshine
slither down the green gloss
of their necks an instant, and are gone.

---

[1] abrupt and disjointed

[2] a man's full-dress coat with tails

Summer hangs drugged from sky to earth
in limpid[3] fathoms[4] of silence:
only warm dark dimples of sound
slide like slow bubbles
from the contented throats.

Raise a casual hand—
with one quick gust
they fountain into air.

---

[3] transparent; clear

[4] units used to measure water depth

Central Park Tourney

by Mildred Weston

ABOUT THE SELECTION

Everyone knows that cars replaced horses for normal, everyday transportation long ago. In "Central Park Tourney," Mildred Weston suggests that they also have replaced the horses used in a more romantic, legendary pastime. As you read the poem, listen for the stops and starts.

Cars
In the Park
With long spear lights
Ride at each other
Like armored knights;
Rush,
Miss the mark,
Pierce the dark,
Dash by!
Another two
Try.

Staged
In the Park
From dusk
To dawn,
The tourney goes on:
Rush,
Miss the mark,
Pierce the dark,
Dash by!
Another two
Try.

whom do you visualize as your reader?

by Linda Pastan

ABOUT THE SELECTION

Linda Pastan (1932–   ) was born in New York, graduated from Radcliffe, and earned two graduate degrees. Although she won a national poetry contest while in college, she stopped writing when she married. When her children entered school, Pastan's husband urged her to return to writing. She has since won numerous awards and grants. The theme of many of her poems is the conflict between daily chores and great ideas; between the housewife and the poet. Pastan has said that many of her poems are inspired by dreams. The following poem, however, grew out of her response to a questionnaire. Pastan was invited, along with other poets, to discuss the creative process. One of the questions the poets were asked serves as the title of the poem.

the humanities 5 section man[1]
who has been sharpening
his red pencil
these twenty years

my mother
who suspected me
of such thoughts
all along

the running back
who after the last touchdown
reads my poems by his locker
instead of the sports page

---

[1] an instructor in the humanities department of a college or university

A Noiseless Patient Spider

by Walt Whitman

ABOUT THE SELECTION

Walt Whitman (1819–1892) is considered one of America's greatest poets. In addition to writing about government and democracy, much of his poetry focuses on themes such as the beauty of friendship and the importance of the self, death, and immortality. The poem below illustrates his characteristic optimism toward life. For more information about Whitman, see About This Poet at the beginning of this unit.

A noiseless patient spider,
I mark'd where on a little promontory[1] it stood isolated,
Mark'd how to explore the vacant vast surrounding,
It launch'd forth filament,[2] filament, filament, out of itself,
Ever unreeling them, ever tirelessly speeding them.

And you O my soul where you stand,
Surrounded, detached, in measureless oceans of space,
Ceaselessly musing, venturing, throwing, seeking the spheres to
    connect them,
Till the bridge you will need be form'd, till the ductile[3] anchor
    hold,
Till the gossamer[4] thread you fling catch somewhere, O, my
    soul.

---

[1] a high ridge of land or rock jutting into water

[2] a fine or thinly spun thread or fiber

[3] easily molded or shaped

[4] sheer; light; delicate

Running It Backward

by John N. Morris

ABOUT THE SELECTION

Born in England, John N. Morris (1931–   ) was educated in the United States and served in the Marines, becoming a first lieutenant. He returned to school to earn a doctorate at Columbia University and then became a professor of English. He has taught at Washington University in St. Louis since 1967. His writings include books of poetry, short stories, and literary criticism. As you begin reading "Running It Backward," imagine that you are watching a home movie about memorable events in a friend's life.

A simple flick of the switch
And his familiar figure
Steps back out of the doorway,
Out of the fond familiar arms
That now drop eagerly to her sides.
Backward he rapidly walks
On the crazy pavement
Into his car whose door
Flies into his hand at a gesture;
Expertly staring ahead, he
Reverses quickly out of the picture.

At first it is mildly funny
Watching him perform
With such cheerful address[1]
These difficult backward
Easy forward things.
So when the whiskey
Arises into the bottle
And, smiling,
He refuses his first job
And returns the diploma
With a firm handshake,
We laugh.
                    But suddenly
It is turning serious, we see
That he is going
Where we do not wish to follow.
That smile still on his face
But growing doubtful now,
He is climbing down
Out of his college,
Through algebra and beginning French
Into a taste for Coca-Cola.

Now quickly he falls
Through the grades
Into his shorts
And the birthday parties.
Though a profusion[2] of gifts
Resume their brilliant paper,
There, as the breath returns
To him who gave it
And laughter fades
To pure expectancy,

---

[1] grace in dealing with a situation

[2] abundance; unrestrained plenty

Before the match withdraws
That seemed to lean
To seem to put them out,
Out of the dark the candles come
At once alight.

Here with a flick of the switch
It is time to be stopping,
For looking ahead
We foresee what is true
But improper to be shown:
How, soon, he is going faster,
How he lapses[3] from language
Into helpless tears,
A rage beneath naming
Shaking him as he dwindles;
How, behind his silent scream,
He disappears
In a fury of flapping and clicking
Into the dark and shining
Whirring tiny mouth of the machine.

---

[3] falls from a previous, higher standard

Where You Are

by Jack Anderson

ABOUT THE SELECTION

Jack Anderson (1935–   ) is both a poet and a dance critic who has won awards for both types of writing. Born in Milwaukee, Wisconsin, he graduated from Northwestern University in Evanston, Illinois, and did graduate work in Indiana and California before beginning to write about dance for newspapers and magazines. Anderson has written at least six books each of poetry and nonfiction histories of dance. Some critics note that in many of his poems, such as in "Where You Are," the poem itself is presented as an "art happening."

This is where you are.
Please note.
You are reading a poem
Beginning, "This is where you are."
Now get up
And walk three times around the room,
Then drink from a faucet
(If you can find a faucet).
Do not use a glass.
Stick your mouth directly
Into the stream of water.
Feel the water,
Its coldness, its wetness.

If there is no faucet near you
Or if the water is not potable,[1]
Observe the sky
And whatever may fill it
(in the margin you may write
The names of three things
You see in the sky)
And try to decide
Whether our present condition
Is best described
As peace or war.
What is the difference
Between this and "this"?
Please take note
Of where you are.
Did you really walk around the room
As requested?
Have you written anything in the margin?
Are you sitting, standing,
Or reclining?
You are reading a poem
Which will end,
"Of all this is."
But you are not there yet.
You are here.
You are getting there.
Now explain precisely
What the point
Of all this is.

---

[1] drinkable

Childhood

by Maura Stanton

ABOUT THE SELECTION

Poet and novelist Maura Stanton (1946–   ) was born in Evanston, Illinois, and earned degrees at the Universities of Minnesota and Iowa. One group of poems in her first poetry collection, *Snow on Snow,* was about a real historical person. Stanton received a grant to do research on the woman and then wrote a fictional novel based on her life, called *Molly Companion.* Stanton's poetry and her fiction have won numerous awards. "Childhood" suggests her ability to combine realistic details and puzzling fantasy.

I used to lie on my back, imagining
A reverse house on the ceiling of my house
Where I could walk around in empty rooms
All by myself. There was no furniture
Up there, only a glass globe in the floor,
And knee-high barriers at every door.
The low silled windows opened on blue air.
Nothing hung in the closet; even the kitchen
Seemed immaculate,[1] a place for thought.
I liked to walk across the swirling plaster
Into the parts of the house I couldn't see.
The hum from the other house, now my ceiling,
Reached me only faintly. I'd look up
To find my brothers watching old cartoons,
Or my mother vacuuming the ugly carpet.

---

[1]spotlessly clean

I'd stare amazed at unmade beds, the clutter,
Shoes, half-dressed dolls, the telephone,
Then return dizzily to my perfect floorplan
Where I never spoke or listened to anyone.
I must have turned down the wrong hall,
Or opened a door that locked shut behind me,
For I live on the ceiling now, not the floor.
This is my house, room after empty room.
How do I ever get back to the real house
Where my sisters spill milk, my father calls,
And I am at the table, eating cereal?
I fill my white rooms with furniture,
Hang curtains over the piercing blue outside.
I lie on my back. I strive to look down.
The ceiling is higher than it used to be,
The floor so far away I can't determine
Which room I'm in, which year, which life.

UNDERSTANDING THE POEMS

Record your answers to these questions in your personal literature notebook. Follow the directions for each group.

GROUP 1   Reread the poems in Group 1 to complete these sentences.

Reviewing the Selection

1. The speaker in "Pigeons" is observing the birds during the
   a. summer.
   b. winter.
   c. spring.
   d. fall.

2. The setting of "African Sunrise" is a
   a. lonely seashore.
   b. busy marketplace.
   c. tropical jungle.
   d. desert oasis.

Interpreting the Selection

3. In "African Sunrise" the description of the wind as "Sharp-beaked with yellow/Nipping the bunched date palms . . ." suggests that
   a. a yellow sun is shining on parrots as they fly through the wind.
   b. the wind is blowing through the palms as if pecking at them with beaks.
   c. yellow parrots are piercing through the wind with their sharp beaks.
   d. the air is so hot that it "pecks" at the skin like sharp yellow beaks.

Recognizing How Words Are Used

4. In "Pigeons" the sunlight shining on the feathers of the pigeons' necks is compared to
   a. bubbles.
   b. fountains.
   c. ghosts.
   d. powder.

Appreciating Poetry

5. The mood of "African Sunrise" could best be described as
   a. realistic.
   b. mysterious.
   c. dangerous.
   d. sad.

──────── **GROUP 2**   Reread the poems in Group 2 to complete these sentences.

Reviewing the
Selection

6. The speaker in "A Noiseless Patient Spider" is speaking to
   a. a spider.
   b. the soul of the reader.
   c. an ocean.
   d. the speaker's own soul.

7. In "whom do you visualize as your reader?" the only person the poet does *not* consider is
   a. the poet's mother.
   b. the poet's best friend.
   c. a football player.
   d. a college teacher.

Interpreting the
Selection

8. In "whom do you visualize as your reader?" the list of possible readers is meant to show that
   a. the poet wants anyone and everyone to read her poems.
   b. the poet wants three special friends or relatives to read her poems.
   c. only teachers, mothers, and football players read this poet's poems.
   d. some readers like her poetry better than other readers do.

Recognizing How
Words Are Used

9. In "Central Park Tourney" the phrase "long spear lights" refers to
   a. light poles in the park that are shaped like spears.
   b. traffic signals stopping traffic like spears would stop enemies.
   c. car headlights resembling knights' spears.
   d. magic spears made of light.

Appreciating Poetry

10. The speaker in "A Noiseless Patient Spider" compares the spider's efforts to send its web to a distant point with his or her own efforts to
   a. mark where the spider stands.
   b. connect with somewhere or someone else.
   c. go out into space.
   d. manufacture bridges and anchors.

GROUP 3　Reread the poems in Group 3 to complete these sentences.

Reviewing the Selection

11. The speaker in "Childhood" imagines
   a. having brothers and sisters.
   b. lying on her back.
   c. living on the ceiling of her house.
   d. walking on the ceiling.

12. In the title "Running It Backward," the word *It* refers to a
   a. race in which the runners run backward.
   b. home movie that is run in reverse.
   c. car that is stuck in reverse.
   d. broken machine.

Interpreting the Selection

13. At the end of "Running It Backward" the "flapping and clicking" sounds are made by
   a. someone's loose shoes.
   b. someone in a film.
   c. the film in a projector.
   d. the gears of a projector.

Appreciating Poetry

14. The best word to describe the speaker's tone in "Where You Are" is
   a. serious.
   b. angry.
   c. fearful.
   d. lighthearted.

Recognizing How
Words Are Used

15. In "Running It Backward" the poet describes a match "That seemed to lean /To seem to put" candles out. The best explanation for why the poet uses the word *seem* twice is that

a. he couldn't think of a more colorful verb.

b. *seem* and *lean* are rhyming words.

c. he wanted to stress that the actions only seemed to happen that way.

d. he didn't notice that he used the word twice.

Now check your answers with your teacher. Study the questions you answered incorrectly. What types of questions were they? Talk with your teacher about ways to work on those skills.

What Is a Poem?

During the course of a single day you probably read many different forms of writing. For instance, you might read the headlines of a newspaper, a diagram of a shopping mall, and a science textbook. Each of these forms of writing has a distinct purpose, and its format reflects that purpose. For example, headlines are meant to attract readers' attention and to quickly and clearly convey the messages of newspaper articles. Therefore, they are printed in large, bold type and contain mostly nouns and verbs. A diagram of a mall is meant to help people find different parts of the mall, so it contains a drawing of the mall and words that identify stores, restaurants, and other features. A textbook is intended to express and explain complex ideas and relationships. In order to do this, it uses complete and often descriptive sentences that follow the standard rules of grammar, capitalization, and punctuation.

As with these other types of writing, the form of a poem also reflects its purpose. Like textbooks, some poems may express complex ideas and relationships. Such poems may use complete sentences and may follow certain rules of grammar, capitalization, and punctuation. Like diagrams, other poems may use graphics as well as words to express their meaning. And like newspaper headlines, most poems try to attract readers' attention and convey the poems' messages in as few words as possible.

In order to help you better understand and appreciate poetry, this unit will focus on the following techniques that poets use in their writing:

- Some poets use exact and colorful words that appeal to readers' senses or emotions. They also make unusual comparisons or connections that help readers look at familiar objects or ideas in new ways.

- Some poets use distinct sounds, rhymes, rhythms, and even physical characteristics to catch readers' attention and help them understand a poem's meaning.
- All poets describe particular experiences from their own unique point of view.

LESSON 1

SENSORY IMAGES AND COMPARISONS

Have you ever heard someone describe a piece of prose by saying that it sounded just like poetry? If you have, it's not the rhyme or the rhythm of the piece that evoked that particular comparison but the poetic way in which the writer used words to paint a striking picture, or *image*. Indeed, the use of colorful and descriptive images is one of the most important distinguishing characteristics of most poetry. Poets use images and surprising comparisons to recreate sights, sounds, and experiences. They appeal to readers in a most direct way—through their senses.

A *sensory detail* is a detail that appeals to one or more of the senses. In the poem "African Sunrise" Gertrude May Lutz uses sensory details to create a precise and memorable sensory image. To which senses do the following lines appeal?

Now the camels
Open their beeswax eyes
And raise long necks,
Rutted sound in their throats—
Camels, pock-marking the sand with spread knees,
Lifting the odor of under-body with them.

Even if you've never been to a desert and observed camels, these lines from the poem make you feel as if you've had the experience. The poet appeals to your sense of sight with references to the camels' slowly opening beeswax eyes, their long necks, and the marks their knees make in the sand. She helps you hear the raspy, guttural sound coming from their throats. She helps you smell the odor that escapes when these large, sweaty animals rise from sitting to standing positions. All of these individual details combine to create a full, clear sensory image.

Another characteristic of poetry is the use of unusual comparisons to create mental pictures. In "Pigeons" Richard Kell studies a bird who normally gets little attention. He helps us see the pigeon in a new light by comparing it to other objects that are normally unrelated. For example, how many comparisons can you find in the following lines from the poem?

> They paddle with staccato feet
> in powder-pools of sunlight,
> small blue busybodies
> strutting like fat gentlemen
> with hands clasped
> under their swallowtail coats;
> and, as they stump about,
> their heads like tiny hammers
> tap at imaginary nails
> in non-existent walls.

You may never think of pigeons in the same way again after reading this poem. In it, pigeons are compared to busybodies because of their quick, sharp movements and their persistence in going where they are not welcome. They are compared to fat gentlemen with hands clasped under elegant tailcoats because of the portly shape of their bodies and arrangement of their feathers. The poet looks at their heads jabbing at insects and bread on the ground and sees tiny hammers tapping at non-existent walls. Each of these comparisons causes you to think carefully about the pigeon in a way that you may never have done before and to see its appearance and habits from an unusual point of view. Recalling these images and comparisons the next time you see a flock of

pigeons, you may begin to look at them in an entirely different way.

EXERCISE ①

Reread "Pigeons" and then use what you have learned in this
lesson to answer these questions:

1. To what are the sounds that the pigeons make compared? How
   could you describe that sound without using a comparison?

2. What do the pigeons do at the end of the poem? Describe
   the image that is created in your mind with the words "they
   fountain into air."

Now check your answers with your teacher. Review this
part of the lesson if you don't understand why an answer was
incorrect.

WRITING ON YOUR OWN ①

You have learned that poetry often uses surprising comparisons to help you see things in new ways. In this exercise you
will draw a few comparisons of your own. Follow these steps:

• Think of an inanimate object (a nonliving thing) that you use
  or see every day—perhaps a pencil, a school bus, or a
  cereal box. Now think of a living thing that is like that object
  in some way. Let your imagination run wild. Write a comparison in one or two sentences that explains what these two
  things have in common.
• With three or four other students, brainstorm and list five
  inanimate objects in no particular order. Then list five living
  things, again in no particular order. Next, find as many connections between the inanimate objects and the living things

as possible. For example, if the inanimate object were a telephone and the living thing were a raccoon, possible connections might be that they both have rings and that they both can disturb you with noise in the middle of the night.

- Have one member of the group record all the comparisons and connections. Then share them with the rest of the class. See how creative you can be.

LESSON ② SOUND AND FORM

In most cases, poems look and sound different from prose. Here are some of the ways in which they are different:

- Prose is usually written in sentences that are grouped together in paragraphs. With very few exceptions, poetry is written in lines that are grouped together in *stanzas*.
- In most prose, the writer doesn't care how a paragraph looks in writing. It makes no difference how many lines the paragraph has or where the lines break. In poetry, however, the writer decides exactly how many lines should appear in each stanza and where each line should break. The poet also may decide to use a certain number and pattern of stressed syllables in a line or particular patterns of consonant and vowel sounds in a group of lines.
- Almost all prose follows standard rules of grammar, punctuation, and spelling. In poetry, however, a poet may ignore those rules. In some poems, every line and/or sentence begins with a capital letter. In other poems, there are no capital letters at all. In still other poems, there is little or no punctuation and no complete sentences.

Although the appearance of a poem is often a guide to its organization, the sound of a poem is usually more important to its meaning. Poets use two important patterns of sound: rhythm and rhyme. *Rhythm* is the pattern of sound created by the arrangement of stressed and unstressed syllables. Some rhythms are very regular and obvious, as in this nursery rhyme:

> Twinkle, twinkle, little star,
> How I wonder what you are,

Other rhythms are irregular and more conversational, as in "whom do you visualize as your reader?":

> the running back
> who after the last touchdown
> reads my poems by his locker
> instead of the sports page

Still other rhythms combine different patterns for special effect. For example, read these lines from "Central Park Tourney." Each stressed syllable is marked with an accent (/), while unstressed syllables are marked with this symbol: ∪.

1 Cárs

2 In the Párk

3 With lóng spéar líghts

4 Ríde at éach óther

5 Líke ármored kníghts;

6 Rúsh,

7 Míss the márk,

8 Píerce the dárk,

9 Dásh bý!

In the first five lines, there is at least one unstressed syllable between all the stressed syllables. This pattern gives the lines a rapid flow; it even suggests a gallop in lines 4–5. But at the beginning of line 4 and lines 6 through 9, there is a stressed syllable following the stressed syllable at the end of the preceding line. The reader has to pause momentarily between the two stresses. This automatically suggests the bursts of action that the poem talks about. In line 9, the use of only two syllables, both stressed, emphasizes the force of the action.

Then at the end of each line from line 5 through line 9, there is a punctuation mark that forces the reader to pause and notice each line by itself. Lines 7 and 8 each follow a pattern of one unstressed syllable between two stressed syllables, but line 9 shortens the pattern. That little change makes line 9 move faster, emphasizing the meaning of the words. The poet has used rhythm in this poem to help the reader feel what is being described.

Rhyme, another important pattern of sound, is the repetition of ending sounds, as in the words *park*, *mark*, and *dark* in "Central Park Tourney."

Other patterns of sound in poems are repetitions of all kinds, including these:

- *alliteration*—the repetition of consonant sounds—as in the phrase *vacant vast surrounding* from "A Noiseless Patient Spider"
- *assonance*—the repetition of vowel sounds—as in the phrase *O my soul* from the same poem
- the repetition of whole words or phrases, as in the phrase *filament, filament, filament* in the same poem
- *refrain*—the repetition of the same line or lines—as in these lines, which are repeated at the end of each stanza in "Central Park Tourney":

Rush,
Miss the mark,

Pierce the dark,
Dash by!
Another two
Try.

What is the reason for all this repetition? For one thing, having the same sounds or words come up again holds a poem together. For another, repeated sounds, particularly in rhymes, make a poem easier to remember. In addition, repeating certain words can emphasize an idea or a mood. Look, for example, at the repetition of the word *filament* in "A Noiseless Patient Spider." Seeing and hearing the word three times impresses upon the reader the persistence of the spider as it patiently throws out its filaments over and over and over.

EXERCISE ②

Reread the poems in Group 2. Then use what you have learned in this lesson to answer these questions:

1. How many stanzas are there in "whom do you visualize as your reader"? What similarities can you see among the stanzas? Which one word is repeated in all of the stanzas?

2. Review "A Noiseless Patient Spider." Identify at least two words or phrases that are repeated in stanza 1. In stanza 2, identify a single word that is used three times to link phrases. Besides the examples discussed earlier in this lesson, identify an example of alliteration (two or more words in a phrase that begin with the same consonant sound).

3. In "Central Park Tourney" what other rhymes or near-rhymes do you find in addition to *mark/park/dark?*

Now check your answers with your teacher. Review this part of the lesson if you don't understand why an answer was incorrect.

WRITING ON YOUR OWN ②

Use what you have learned in this lesson to complete the exercise below. Follow these steps:

- Mark the stressed and unstressed syllables in the following words, which come from poems in this unit. After you have finished, compare your work with that of a classmate. Did you both mark the words the same way?

  caravan   staccato   busybodies
  filament   gossamer   touchdown
  imagining   beginning   machine

- In a previous writing exercise you recorded instances of interesting sounds, words, and phrases that you heard in daily life. Now write a short advertisement that uses sounds, words, or phrases for effect. You may write it in the form of a poem or a paragraph. Feel free to use any of the words you recorded earlier or any of the ones listed above.

LESSON ③   AN INTENSE, PERSONAL VIEW

You've probably heard of photographers who take shot after shot of the same model or scene in nature. They are looking for a unique combination of angle, expression, composition, and lighting that will make visible something that no one has seen before. Poets do the same thing, only with words instead of film. Their topics may be familiar, but they present those topics in new lights and from different angles. They can make even the most common objects or ideas seem brand-new, unique, and different.

Look, for example, at "Running It Backward." The poem begins by describing a trick almost everyone has seen many times: running a film backward. At a "simple flick of the switch," the man in the film

Steps back out of the doorway,
Out of the fond familiar arms
That now drop eagerly to her sides.
Backward he rapidly walks
On the crazy pavement
Into his car whose door
Flies into his hand at a gesture;

At first, imagining the view of a man's actions in reverse is familiar. As we read the first part of the poem, we are inclined to smile. We barely notice that the man has gone from simply walking backward to returning his diploma. The poem's tone and mood begin to shift.

But suddenly
It is turning serious, we see
That he is going
Where we do not wish to follow.

The mood has changed from humor to foreboding, to an uneasy feeling that something bad is going to happen. The man is now "climbing down" out of college and falling "Through the grades" to an early birthday party. The speaker describes the reverse of the boy's blowing out the candles, and we are reminded of something mysterious and somewhat frightening:

There, as the breath returns
To him who gave it
And laughter fades
To pure expectancy,
Before the match withdraws
That seemed to lean
To seem to put them out,
Out of the dark the candles come
At once alight.

The poem marches on to the logical outcome of this backward motion—the man, now a boy, will go back to being an infant and then still further back:

> We foresee what is true
> But improper to be shown:

The poem ends with the man/boy/infant disappearing "Into the dark and shining/Whirring tiny mouth of the machine." At first it might seem that this poem is about nothing more than running a film backward on a projector. However, after reading it more carefully, you might begin to think about it differently. For example, you might put yourself in the film and begin to wonder where and who you were before now. You might wonder what you will become. These questions certainly aren't new. By using the idea of running your life backward on a projector, however, the poet makes you look at your life from a new and different angle.

EXERCISE ③

Reread the poems in Group 3. Then use what you have learned in this lesson to answer these questions:

1. In "Where You Are" what does the speaker say the reader is doing? What are some of the sensory adventures that the speaker invites the reader to experience? Why do you suppose the poem talks about both reading a poem and appreciating sensory experiences? Explain what you think is significant about these lines:

> Please take note
> Of where you are.

2. What activity does the speaker in "Childhood" describe? What problem does the speaker encounter with this activity? Use your own words to describe the mood of the poem—that is, the way it makes you feel. Have you ever had a problem that left you with a feeling similar to this one? How was your problem like the speaker's problem?

Now check your answers with your teacher. Review this part of the lesson if you don't understand why an answer was incorrect.

WRITING ON YOUR OWN ③

In this exercise you will begin to think about topics that you could use in a poem of your own. Follow these steps:

- Make a list of several issues and beliefs that you feel very strongly about—for example, the importance of having friends and family, taking on certain responsibilities, caring for the environment, and so on. After you review your list, narrow it down to just two issues or beliefs.
- For each of those items, list two or more situations that would cause you to consider your feelings or beliefs. For example, if you believe that charity toward the homeless is essential, a situation in which you would have to consider your belief would be when a man approaches you and asks for a donation. Or if you are concerned with racial justice, reading an article in the newspaper might cause you to focus on the problem and review your feelings about it.
- Save your notes to use in the final writing exercise.

DISCUSSION GUIDES

1. The speakers in many of Walt Whitman's poems speak with strength, confidence, and good humor. With another student, locate some more poems by Whitman and choose two that you particularly like. Practice reading them aloud and expressing the speakers' qualities. Then take turns presenting your oral readings to the rest of the class.

2. With a small group of classmates, review the poems in this unit. Which poems are particularly appealing to you? Individually, rank the poems from 1 to 8, with 1 being your favorite and 8 being your least favorite. Then get together with the group and share your lists and the reasons for your choices. Don't be surprised to find that the poem you like least is someone else's favorite. Poetry appreciation, like poetry writing, is very personal and individual.

3. Because poetry is highly personal, you probably had opinions about it before you began reading this book. You may have enjoyed poetry before this, or you may have decided that it is not your favorite form of writing. Did reading the poetry and studying the techniques in this first unit make you want to read more poetry? Why or why not? Does a particular poet's work—either one in this unit or any other—appeal to you? After discussing these questions with your class, work together to create a questionnaire containing three to five questions about attitudes toward poetry. Make sure your questions can be answered with the word *yes* or *no* or by marking numbers from *1* to *10.* Have everyone in the class answer the questionnaire, and then report the results. At the end of this book, administer the questionnaire again to see if your classmates' attitudes toward poetry and their understanding of what makes a good poem have changed.

WRITE A PERSONAL POEM

In this unit you have been introduced to different aspects of poetry. Now you will write your own poem, using what you have learned about poetry so far.

Follow these steps to write your poem. If you have questions about the writing process, refer to Using the Writing Process on page 232.

- Assemble and review the work you did for all the writing exercises in this unit: 1) examples of the use of poetry in everyday life, 2) creative comparisons between inanimate objects and living things, 3) analyses of the stresses in words and an ad that uses repetition, 4) topics you care about and situations when you might think deeply about them.
- Look over the issues and situations you developed for Writing on Your Own 3. Which issue and situation do you feel most strongly about? Make that issue and situation the subject of your poem.
- Jot down details about the situation and then answer questions such as these: Would a comparison help you describe your idea or situation more effectively? If so, what would that comparison be? Can you use the repetition of sounds, words, or phrases to state your ideas more clearly or forcefully? Do you want your poem to rhyme? What are your feelings as you experience or think through the situation? How could you best convey those feelings to your readers?
- Write your poem. Include details or comparisons that paint a clear picture of people or things involved in the situation. Be consistent in your use of rhyme and rhythm—or your decision not to use them. Try to include repetition at least once.
- Ask a classmate to read your poem. Are the message and feelings you are trying to communicate clear? If you have included a comparison, can he or she tell what two things are being compared? Make any neccessary changes. Then rewrite your poem.
- Proofread your final poem for spelling and grammar errors. Save it in your writing portfolio.

Speakers in Poetry

Grass
by Carl Sandburg

Bee! I'm Expecting You!
by Emily Dickinson

Miniver Cheevy
by Edwin Arlington Robinson

The Runaway
by Robert Frost

On a Night of Snow
by Elizabeth Coatsworth

I'm Nobody! Who are you?
by Emily Dickinson

My Father Is a Simple Man
by Luis Omar Salinas

The Highwayman
by Alfred Noyes

Molly Means
by Margaret Walker

INTRODUCTION

ABOUT THE LESSONS

When poets write poems, they are like actors playing different roles. They take on new identities and speak in a variety of voices. For example, besides speaking as themselves, they may speak from the point of view of familiar or imaginary people and animals or even inanimate objects. The character whose words you read in a poem is called the *speaker*.

This unit will focus on the speakers in nine poems. The poems are divided into three groups. The poems in Group 1 will help you focus on identifying the speaker and the intended audience of each poem. The poems in Group 2 will help you hear the speakers' voices as they talk to themselves or others. The poems in Group 3 will help you focus on the role of the speaker in a narrative poem.

WRITING: DEVELOPING A STORY FOR A POEM

At the end of this unit, you will write a poem that tells a story. Begin developing that story by following these steps:

- Think of actual events in your life that have been exciting, funny, surprising, or significant in some way. Make a list of those events that you think would make good stories.
- If you do not wish to write about events from your own life, make a list of events that you have read, seen, or heard about. The events can be real or imaginary.
- Save your list to use in later writing exercises.

ABOUT THIS POET

Emily Dickinson (1830–1886) is considered to be one of America's major poets. Her family, longtime residents of New England, came from a strict Puritan background. Dickinson was educated at Amherst Academy and Mount Holyoke Female Seminary. As a young girl she was said to be outgoing and friendly, but as she grew older she retreated more and more into the private world of her family home until she rarely went out at all. Her main contact with her few close friends in the outside world was through the approximately 10,000 letters that she sent them. Always dressing in white, she lived on the second floor of her home and wrote poetry. Nearly 2,000 poems and parts of poems were found in her rooms after her death.

During Dickinson's life only seven or eight of her poems were published, and they were published anonymously. After her death, however, her relatives and admirers gathered her poems and published some of them in *Poems*, a volume that enjoyed immediate success. Today, audiences and critics respect Dickinson's mastery of figurative language, her use of precise words with rich connotations, the complexity of her rhythms and rhymes, and her original and personal way of looking at basic issues like life, death, and love.

AS YOU READ

As you read each poem in this unit, ask yourself these questions about the speaker:

- Who is the speaker (or speakers) in this poem? What do each speaker's words reveal about him or her?
- Whom is the speaker (or speakers) addressing in this poem?
- In a narrative poem, how does the speaker's point of view affect the way the story is told?

Grass

by Carl Sandburg

ABOUT THE SELECTION

Carl Sandburg (1878–1967) was born in Galesburg, Illinois. He wrote many poems that expressed the thoughts of common people, using conversational language and free verse. In 1940 Sandburg won the Pulitzer Prize for his biography of Abraham Lincoln, and in 1951 he won again for his book called *Complete Poems.* Sandburg wrote the following poem during World War I, after hearing that tens of thousands of soldiers had been killed at Ypres and Verdun. In recordings of the poem made during World War II, Sandburg added the location name "Stalingrad" to the list of battlefields. (The Germans attacked Stalingrad, and the Soviets successfully counterattacked. The Battle of Stalingrad is now viewed as the major turning point of World War II.) Notice the relentless strength of the speaker's voice in this poem.

Pile the bodies high at Austerlitz and Waterloo.
Shovel them under and let me work—
        I am the grass; I cover all.

And pile them high at Gettysburg
And pile them high at Ypres and Verdun.
Shovel them under and let me work.
Two years, ten years, and passengers ask the conductor:
        What place is this?
        Where are we now?

        I am the grass.
        Let me work.

Bee! I'm Expecting You!

by Emily Dickinson

ABOUT THE SELECTION

Emily Dickinson (1830–1886) was born in Amherst, Massachusetts, and lived most of her life on the second floor of her family home there. Although only a few of her poems were published during her lifetime, years after her death she has been recognized as one of America's finest poets. Her poems, including the one you are about to read, express her individualism and unusual perspectives on life. For more information about Dickinson, see About This Poet at the beginning of this unit.

Bee! I'm expecting you!
Was saying Yesterday
To Somebody you know
That you were due—

The Frogs got Home Last Week—
Are settled, and at work—
Birds, mostly back—
The Clover warm and thick—

You'll get my Letter by
The seventeenth; Reply
Or better, be with me—
Yours, Fly.

Miniver Cheevy

by Edwin Arlington Robinson

ABOUT THE SELECTION

Edwin Arlington Robinson (1869–1935) was born in Gardiner, a small town in Maine. In many of his poems, this three-time Pulitzer Prize winner focused on the lives of inhabitants of a town similar to Gardiner, which he named Tilbury Town. A number of later poets, including Robert Frost, claim to have been influenced by Robinson's writing. How is the speaker in this poem different from the others in this group?

Miniver Cheevy, child of scorn,
    Grew lean while he assailed the seasons;
He wept that he was ever born,
    And he had reasons.

Miniver loved the days of old
    When swords were bright and steeds were prancing;
The vision of a warrior bold
    Would set him dancing.

Miniver sighed for what was not,
    And dreamed, and rested from his labors;
He dreamed of Thebes[1] and Camelot,[2]
    And Priam's[3] neighbors.

---

[1] ancient city in Egypt

[2] site of King Arthur's court

[3] king of Troy during the Trojan War

Miniver mourned the ripe renown
> That made so many a name so fragrant;
He mourned Romance, now on the town,
> And Art, a vagrant.

Miniver loved the Medici,[4]
> Albeit[5] he had never seen one;
He would have sinned incessantly
> Could he have been one.

Miniver cursed the commonplace
> And eyed a khaki suit with loathing;
He missed the medieval grace
> Of iron clothing.

Miniver scorned the gold he sought,
> But sore annoyed was he without it;
Miniver thought, and thought, and thought,
> And thought about it.

Miniver Cheevy, born too late,
> Scratched his head and kept on thinking;
Miniver coughed, and called it fate,
> And kept on drinking.

---

[4] family in medieval Italy known for its power and intrigue

[5] although

The Runaway

by Robert Frost

ABOUT THE SELECTION

Although Robert Frost (1874–1963) was born in California, he is usually associated with New England. In fact, he did do some farming in New England for about ten years before establishing his fame as a poet. In "The Runaway," he speaks with authority about a sight that may be familiar to farmers in cold regions—a young colt experiencing its first winter. For more information about Frost, see About This Poet at the beginning of Unit 4.

Once when the snow of the year was beginning to fall,
We stopped by a mountain pasture to say, "Whose colt?"
A little Morgan[1] had one forefoot on the wall,
The other curled at his breast. He dipped his head
And snorted at us. And then he had to bolt.
We heard the miniature thunder where he fled,
And we saw him, or thought we saw him, dim and grey
Like a shadow against the curtain of falling flakes.
"I think the little fellow's afraid of the snow.
He isn't winter-broken. It isn't play
With the little fellow at all. He's running away.
I doubt if even his mother could tell him, 'Sakes,
It's only weather.' He'd think she didn't know!
Where is his mother? He can't be out alone."

---

[1] a type of horse

And now he comes again with a clatter of stone,
And mounts the wall again with whited eyes
And all his tail that isn't hair up straight.
He shudders his coat as if to throw off flies.
"Whoever it is that leaves him out so late,
When other creatures have gone to stall and bin,
Ought to be told to come and take him in."

On a Night of Snow

by Elizabeth Coatsworth

ABOUT THE SELECTION

Elizabeth Coatsworth (1893–1986) was born in Buffalo, New York. She traveled widely, especially in Asia. Although Coatsworth wrote poetry, novels, and adult short stories, she probably is known best for her children's books. In fact, she won the Newbery Medal in 1931 for her Japanese-inspired book *The Cat Who Went to Heaven.* In the following poem Coatsworth imagines a conversation between two characters who look at life from different perspectives.

Cat, if you go outdoors you must walk in the snow.
You will come back with little white shoes on your feet,
Little white slippers of snow that have heels of sleet.
Stay by the fire, my Cat. Lie still, do not go.
See how the flames are leaping and hissing low.
I will bring you a saucer of milk like a marguerite,[1]
So white and so smooth, so spherical and so sweet.
Stay with me, Cat. Outdoors the wild winds blow.

Outdoors the wild winds blow, Mistress, and dark is the night.
Strange voices cry in the trees, intoning strange lore,
And more than cats move, lit by our eyes' green light,
On silent feet where the meadow grasses hang hoar[2]—
Mistress, there are portents[3] abroad of magic and might,
And things that are yet to be done. Open the door!

---

[1] flower

[2] frost

[3] omens; things that foreshadow coming events

46

I'm Nobody! Who are you?

by Emily Dickinson

ABOUT THE SELECTION

Emily Dickinson is discussed in About This Poet at the beginning of this unit. In this poem she may be speaking for herself. Read it and decide if you would rather be Somebody or Nobody.

I'm Nobody! Who are you?
Are you—Nobody—Too?
Then there's a pair of us?
Don't tell! they'd advertise—
        you know!

How dreary—to be—
        Somebody!
How public—like a Frog—
To tell one's name—the
        livelong June—
To an admiring Bog!

My Father Is a Simple Man

by Luis Omar Salinas

ABOUT THE SELECTION   Luis Omar Salinas (1937–   ) was born in Texas but spent the first few years of his life in Mexico. When he was nine, he was sent to live with relatives in California. He has won a number of prizes for his poetry, which often focuses on the problems of Mexican Americans, including poverty and a sense of not feeling welcome in mainstream American society. As you read this poem, look for the speaker's attitude toward his or her father.

I walk to town with my father
to buy a newspaper. He walks slower
than I do so I must slow up.
The street is filled with children.
We argue about the price
of pomegranates, I convince
him it is the fruit of scholars.
He has taken me on this journey
and it's been lifelong.
He's sure I'll be healthy
so long as I eat more oranges,
and tells me the orange
has seeds and so is perpetual;
and we too will come back
like the orange trees.
I ask him what he thinks
about death and he says
he will gladly face it when

it comes but won't jump
out in front of a car.
I'd gladly give my life
for this man with a sixth
grade education, whose kindness
and patience are true . . .
The truth of it is, he's the scholar,
and when the bitter-hard reality
comes at me like a punishing
evil stranger, I can always
remember that here was a man
who was a worker and provider,
who learned the simple facts
in life and lived by them,
who held no pretense.[1]
And when he leaves without
benefit of fanfare or applause
I shall have learned what little
there is about greatness.

---

[1] insincerity; false show; fakery

The Highwayman

by Alfred Noyes

ABOUT THE SELECTION

Alfred Noyes (1880–1958), a British writer of poetry, biographies, essays, and novels, often chose to write about fantasy and nature. He is said to have written "The Highwayman" in only two days when he was 24. The poem is set in England at a time when robbers called highwaymen set upon unsuspecting travelers and took their money and possessions. The redcoats referred to in the poem were charged with capturing these criminals.

Part One

The wind was a torrent of darkness among the gusty trees.
The moon was a ghostly galleon[1] tossed upon cloudy seas.
The road was a ribbon of moonlight over the purple moor,
And the highwayman came riding—
      Riding—riding—
The highwayman came riding, up to the old inn door.

He'd a French cocked-hat on his forehead, a bunch of lace at
   his chin,
A coat of the claret velvet, and breeches of brown doeskin.
They fitted with never a wrinkle. His boots were up to the
   thigh.
And he rode with a jeweled twinkle,
      His pistol butts a-twinkle,
His rapier hilt[2] a-twinkle, under the jeweled sky.

---

[1] Spanish sailing ship

[2] the handle of a rapier, which is a kind of sword

Over the cobbles he clattered and clashed in the dark innyard.
He tapped with his whip on the shutters, but all was locked
    and barred.
He whistled a tune to the window, and who should be waiting
    there
But the landlord's black-eyed daughter,
        Bess, the landlord's daughter,
Plaiting³ a dark red love knot into her long black hair.

And dark in the dark old innyard a stable wicket creaked
Where Tim the ostler⁴ listened. His face was white and peaked.
His eyes were hollows of madness, his hair like moldy hay,
But he loved the landlord's daughter,
        The landlord's red-lipped daughter.
Dumb as a dog he listened, and he heard the robber say—

"One kiss, my bonny sweetheart, I'm after a prize to-night,
But I shall be back with the yellow gold before the morning
    light;
Yet, if they press me sharply, and harry⁵ me through the day
Then look for me by moonlight,
        Watch for me by moonlight,
I'll come to thee by moonlight, though hell should bar the
    way."

He rose upright in the stirrups. He scarce could reach her
    hand.
But she loosened her hair in the casement. His face burnt
    like a brand
As the black cascade of perfume came tumbling over his
    breast;

----

³ braiding

⁴ stable worker in charge of handling horses

⁵ bother with constant attacks

And he kissed its waves in the moonlight,
    (O, sweet black waves in the moonlight!)
Then he tugged at his rein in the moonlight, and galloped
    away to the west.

Part Two

He did not come in the dawning. He did not come at noon;
And out of the tawny sunset, before the rise of the moon,
When the road was a gypsy's ribbon, looping the purple moor,
A redcoat troop came marching—
    Marching—marching—
King George's men came marching, up to the old inn door.

They said no word to the landlord. They drank his ale instead.
But they gagged his daughter, and bound her, to the foot of
    her narrow bed.
Two of them knelt at her casement, with muskets at their
    side!
There was death at every window;
    And hell at one dark window;
For Bess could see, through her casement, the road that he
    would ride.

They had tied her up to attention, with many a sniggering[6]
    jest.
They had bound a musket beside her, with the muzzle
    beneath her breast!
"Now, keep good watch!" and they kissed her. She heard the
    doomed man say—
Look for me by moonlight;
    Watch for me by moonlight;
I'll come to thee by moonlight, though hell should bar the
    way!

------

[6] snickering; laughing

She twisted her hands behind her; but all the knots held
    good!
She writhed her hands till her fingers were wet with sweat or
    blood!
They stretched and strained in the darkness, and the hours
    crawled by like years,
Till, now, on the stroke of midnight,
       Cold, on the stroke of midnight,
The tip of one finger touched it! The trigger at least was hers!

The tip of one finger touched it. She strove no more for the
    rest.
Up, she stood up to attention, with the muzzle beneath her
    breast.
She would not risk their hearing; she would not strive again;
For the road lay bare in the moonlight;
       Blank and bare in the moonlight;
And the blood of her veins, in the moonlight, throbbed to her
    love's refrain.

Tlot-tlot; tlot-tlot! Had they heard it? The horsehoofs ringing
    clear;
Tlot-tlot, tlot-tlot, in the distance? Were they deaf that they did
    not hear?
Down the ribbon of moonlight, over the brow of the hill,
The highwayman came riding—
       Riding—riding—
The redcoats looked to their priming![7] She stood up, straight
    and still.

---

[7] explosive that sets off the charge in a firearm

Tlot-tlot, in the frosty silence! *Tlot-tlot*, in the echoing night!
Nearer he came and nearer. Her face was like a light.
Her eyes grew wide for a moment; she drew one last deep
    breath,
Then her finger moved in the moonlight,
      Her musket shattered the moonlight,
Shattered her breast in the moonlight and warned him—with
    her death.

He turned. He spurred to the west; he did not know who stood
Bowed, with her head o'er the musket, drenched with her own
    blood!
Not till the dawn he heard it, and his face grew gray to hear
How Bess, the landlord's daughter,
      The landlord's black-eyed daughter,
Had watched for her love in the moonlight, and died in the
    darkness there.

Back, he spurred like a madman, shouting a curse to the sky,
With the white road smoking behind him and his rapier
    brandished high.
Blood-red were his spurs in the golden noon; wine-red was his
    velvet coat;
When they shot him down on the highway,
      Down like a dog on the highway,
And he lay in his blood on the highway, with a bunch of lace
    at his throat.

. . . .

And still of a winter's night, they say, when the wind is in
    the trees,
When the moon is a ghostly galleon tossed upon cloudy
    seas,
When the road is a ribbon of moonlight over the purple moor,
A highwayman comes riding—
      Riding—riding—
A highwayman comes riding, up to the old inn door.

Over the cobbles he clatters and clangs in the dark innyard.
He taps with his whip on the shutters, but all is locked and
* barred.*
He whistles a tune to the window, and who should be
* waiting there*
But the landlord's black-eyed daughter,
*   Bess, the landlord's daughter,*
Plaiting a dark red love knot into her long black hair.

Molly Means

by Margaret Walker

ABOUT THE SELECTION

Margaret Walker was born in Alabama in 1915. She earned both a master's degree and a doctorate from the University of Iowa. In 1942 she won the Yale Young Poets Award for her first volume of poetry, *For My People,* from which the following poem is taken. In addition to poetry, she has written the historical novel *Jubilee,* essays, and a biography of fellow African-American writer Richard Wright. Now sit back and enjoy a good ghost story about a New Orleans sorceress. Take time to read the story with expression and rhythm.

Old Molly Means was a hag and a witch;
Chile of the devil, the dark, and sitch.
Her heavy hair hung thick in ropes
And her blazing eyes was black as pitch.
Imp at three and wench at 'leben
She counted her husbands to the number seben.
  O Molly, Molly, Molly Means
  There goes the ghost of Molly Means.

Some say she was born with a veil on her face
So she could look through unnatchal space
Through the future and through the past
And charm a body or an evil place
And every man could well despise
The evil look in her coal black eyes.
  Old Molly, Molly, Molly Means
  Dark is the ghost of Molly Means.

And when the tale begun to spread
Of evil and of holy dread:
Her black-hand arts and her evil powers
How she cast her spells and called the dead,
The younguns was afraid at night
And the farmers feared their crops would blight.
    Old Molly, Molly, Molly Means
    Cold is the ghost of Molly Means.

Then one dark day she put a spell
On a young gal-bride just come to dwell
In the lane just down from Molly's shack
And when her husband come riding back
His wife was barking like a dog
And on all fours like a common hog.
    O Molly, Molly, Molly Means
    Where is the ghost of Molly Means?

The neighbors come and they went away
And said she'd die before break of day
But her husband held her in his arms
And swore he'd break the wicked charms,
He'd search all up and down the land
And turn the spell on Molly's hand.
    O Molly, Molly, Molly Means
    Sharp is the ghost of Molly Means.

So he rode all day and he rode all night
And at the dawn he come in sight
Of a man who said he could move the spell
And cause the awful thing to dwell
On Molly Means, to bark and bleed
Till she died at the hands of her evil deed.
    Old Molly, Molly, Molly Means
    This is the ghost of Molly Means.

Sometimes at night through the shadowy trees
She rides along on a winter breeze.
You can hear her holler and whine and cry.
Her voice is thin and her moan is high,
And her cackling laugh or her barking cold
Bring terror to the young and old.
   O Molly, Molly, Molly Means
   Lean is the ghost of Molly Means.

UNDERSTANDING THE POEMS

Record your answers to these questions in your personal literature notebook. Follow the directions for each group.

GROUP 1

Reread the poems in Group 1 to complete these sentences.

Reviewing the Selection

1. The speaker in "Bee! I'm Expecting You!" is communicating his or her message in a
a. song.
b. telegram.
c. telephone.
d. letter.

2. Miniver Cheevy would rather have been living in
a. the future.
b. the time of knights and their ladies.
c. pioneer days.
d. a different city in America.

Interpreting the Selection

3. The speaker in "Grass" sees the hundreds of bodies that are slowly being covered and feels
a. sorrowful.
b. indifferent.
c. proud.
d. angry.

Recognizing How Words Are Used

4. The speaker's choice of words in "The Runaway" creates a mood that could be described as
a. ridiculous.
b. suspicious.
c. concerned.
d. frightening.

Appreciating Poetry

5. The speaker in "Grass" mentions a number of battles fought at different times and places to emphasize that
a. you can visit interesting battlefields in many locations.
b. he knows a great deal about history.
c. grass grows in both Europe and America.
d. humans seem to be drawn to violence and bloodshed.

GROUP 2 Reread the poems in Group 2 to complete these sentences.

Reviewing the Selection

6. The first speaker in "On a Night of Snow" wants the cat to stay inside because
a. it is too cold and snowy outside.
b. he or she is afraid the cat will get lost.
c. he or she knows that cats need to feel safe.
d. it is too much trouble to clean up after a wet cat.

7. The second speaker in "On a Night of Snow" wants to go outside for all the following reasons *except* that
a. the wild winds excite it.
b. it enjoys the sensation of wet and icy paws.
c. it likes danger.
d. it feels that the night is magical.

Interpreting the Selection

8. In "My Father Is a Simple Man" the speaker's relationship with his or her father is one of
a. pity and sympathy.
b. distrust and anger.
c. regret and shame.
d. love and respect.

Recognizing How Words Are Used

9. In "I'm Nobody! Who are you?" the word *Nobody* refers to a
a. person who is not well-known and famous.
b. person who has no self-esteem.
c. spirit, like a ghost, with no physical body.
d. person who refuses to give his or her name to strangers.

10. It is likely that the poet's purposes in writing "I'm Nobody! Who are you?" include all of these reasons *except* to
   a. criticize people who need constant public acclaim.
   b. ridicule frogs and other animals who make loud noises.
   c. explain why she has chosen to live quietly and not publish her poems.
   d. share her feelings about fame.

GROUP 3   Reread the poems in Group 3 to complete these sentences.

Reviewing the Selection

11. The husband in "Molly Means" knows that his wife is under a spell when one day he finds her
   a. barking like a dog.
   b. dying for no reason.
   c. laughing uncontrollably.
   d. eating like a hog.

12. The husband fights back at Molly Means by
   a. killing her with his bare hands.
   b. casting a spell on her himself.
   c. finding a man to turn the spell back on Molly.
   d. gathering neighbors together and driving her away.

Interpreting the Selection

13. In "The Highwayman" the redcoats wait for the highwayman at the old inn that night because
   a. he has a habit of visiting there frequently.
   b. they hear him tell Bess he will be back that night.
   c. the landlord doesn't want his daughter near the highwayman.
   d. Tim the ostler tells them of the conversation he overhears.

Appreciating Poetry

14. The mood of "Molly Means" could be described as
   a. humorous and satirical.
   b. weird and frightening.
   c. respectful and cautious.
   d. practical and matter-of-fact.

Recognizing How Words Are Used

15. *Onomatopoeia* is the use of words that sound like their meanings. An example of onomatopoeia is found in this line from "The Highwayman":

a. His rapier hilt a-twinkle, under the jeweled sky.

b. The road was a ribbon of moonlight over the purple moor,

c. *Tlot-tlot; tlot-tlot!* Had they heard it? The horsehoofs ringing

d. His eyes were hollows of madness, his hair like moldy hay,

Now check your answers with your teacher. Study the questions you answered incorrectly. What types of questions were they? Talk with your teacher about ways to work on those skills.

Speakers in Poetry

You know that the speaker in a poem is the character whose voice you hear. This does not necessarily mean, however, that the speaker is the poet. This is because in many cases, poets take on different personalities to explain new or unusual points of view or to encourage readers to think about objects or ideas in new ways.

To understand any poem, it is essential that you understand who its speaker is. For example, you may wonder why the speaker of a particular poem focuses on the taste of wood or the feel of different fabrics until you discover that the speaker is a termite or a tailor. In addition to identifying the speaker, it is often helpful to identify the poet's intended *audience*—that is, the person or people that the poet is addressing.

The following lessons focus on the speakers in selected poems. In each of these poems, the speaker plays an important role in communicating the message of the poem. A poet may use techniques such as the following to help readers recognize both the speaker and the message of a particular poem:

1. The poet may write from the point of view of another person, character, animal, or inanimate object.

2. The poet may use a monologue (words spoken by only one speaker) or a dialogue (words spoken by more than one speaker) to communicate the message of the poem.

3. The poet may create a speaker who narrates a poem's story from the first-person or third-person point of view.

LESSON 1 LEARNING ABOUT THE SPEAKER

When you listen to a speech, you know who the speaker is and you can be fairly confident that the speaker is voicing his or her own opinions. When you read a newspaper letter to the editor, you know that the speaker is the person who has signed the letter and that this person is voicing his or her opinions. These forms of communication are fairly straightforward and uncomplicated. However, when you read a poem, identifying the speaker can be more difficult. The poet may have been wondering what it would be like to be an eagle or a park bench or the President of the United States and may have decided to write from one of those points of view. When a poet speaks as another person, character, animal, or object, we say that he or she is taking on a different *persona,* or speaking with a different voice and from a different point of view. You learn about the persona of the speaker through what he or she says and the way he or she says it.

Sometimes the speaker is obvious because the poet clearly identifies him or her. For example, the poem "Grass" begins with a shocking command to "pile the bodies high at Austerlitz and Waterloo." The speaker goes on to instruct the audience to "shovel them under and let me work." A person saying these words would be considered heartless and cold, but the poet identifies the speaker in the third line of the poem—"I am the grass; I cover all." At that point we understand why the speaker seems so indifferent to the horror and so single-minded in accomplishing its goal. Grass is a natural element which has no feelings; it doesn't care what or whom it must cover. We are reminded that it is only humans who can recognize the sorrow and waste that wars cause and only humans who can work to change the world.

In "Bee! I'm Expecting You!" Emily Dickinson keeps you waiting until the last line of the poem before she identifies the speaker. However, she lets you know whom the speaker is addressing in the first line when she writes "Bee! I'm expecting you!" The first time you read this line you probably wondered who would be talking to a bee. By the time you reached the last line—"Yours, Fly"—you found the answer. Many readers feel compelled to reread the entire poem, this time knowing who is speaking, and appreciating the way the poet has created a friendly, informal tone befitting a letter to a friend. This imaginary and fanciful letter helps us appreciate the invisible, natural societies all around us that we have a tendency to ignore as we go about our daily business. By using a fly as the speaker, Dickinson helps us take notice of the natural signs that announce the coming of spring.

In both "Grass" and "Bee! I'm Expecting You!" the speaker uses the *first-person point of view* and describes the action using the pronouns *I* and *me*. The speaker in "Miniver Cheevy," on the other hand, describes the action from the *third-person point of view*, using the pronouns *he* and *his*. In this poem, the speaker could be the poet himself, although we can't know for sure. In any case, the speaker shows his or her attitude toward Miniver Cheevy by the details he or she includes:

> Miniver loved the days of old
>   When swords were bright and steeds were prancing;
> The vision of a warrior bold
>   Would set him dancing.
>
> Miniver Cheevy, born too late,
>   Scratched his head and kept on thinking;
> Miniver coughed, and called it fate.
>   And kept on drinking.

The speaker clearly does not respect Miniver but instead sees him as a foolish complainer, longing for the return of romance and wasting his life while he waits. You, as the audience, see Miniver through the speaker's eyes and therefore probably feel the same scorn for him that the speaker does.

The speaker guides the reader into the world of a poem. Once you know who the speaker is and what his or her attitudes are, you can better understand the poem.

EXERCISE (1)

Reread "The Runaway" by Robert Frost. Then use what you have learned in this lesson to answer these questions:

1. What can you guess about the personality of the speaker from the way he or she uses words and from what he or she focuses on?

2. How does the speaker feel toward the young horse? Give reasons for your answer.

3. The speaker in this poem has a conversational and friendly tone. Identify some words and phrases in the poem that help to create this tone.

Now check your answers with your teacher. Review this part of the lesson if you don't understand why an answer was incorrect.

WRITING ON YOUR OWN (1)

In the previous writing exercise you listed possible events that could become a story told in a poem. Now you will make some decisions about the speaker in your poem. Follow these steps:

• Choose the story line that appeals to you most. Briefly outline the major events in your chosen story. The story need not be complete at this point. You will have a chance to add to it and refine it later.

• Think about the speaker who will tell this story to your audience. The speaker could be a character or an object in your story and telling it from the first-person point of view, or the speaker could be outside the story and telling it from the third-person point of view. Write a short paragraph explaining who your speaker is and why you chose him, her, or it.

LESSON 2   SPEAKERS IN MONOLOGUES AND DIALOGUES

Have you ever caught yourself talking to yourself? You might ask, "Where did I put my keys?" or you might say, "I wish I hadn't eaten that last piece of pizza." You don't really expect to hear an answer or a comment in return. You are merely engaging in a *monologue*, a speech involving only one person—yourself. Many poets use monologues also. In poems that are monologues, the speaker is one person, animal, or object who is speaking to the audience.

"My Father Is a Simple Man" by Luis Omar Salinas is an example of a monologue. The speaker, who could be the poet but may be another person or character, is recalling a trip to town with his father:

> I walk to town with my father
> to buy a newspaper. He walks slower
> than I do so I must slow up.
> The street is filled with children.
> We argue about the price
> of pomegranates, I convince
> him it is the fruit of scholars.
> He has taken me on this journey
> and it's been lifelong.

For some reason, this particular trip is significant to the speaker. We hear small details about the street, we learn of an argument about pomegranates, and later in the poem we find out what the father thinks about death. Finally, the speaker seems to understand why he or she has chosen to remember this trip: Reflecting upon this seemingly unimportant event, the speaker has come to realize the impact that the father has had on the speaker's life and the intense feelings of love that the memory has brought forth. We read this monologue and become witnesses to the speaker's discoveries:

The truth of it is, he's the scholar,
and when the bitter-hard reality
comes at me like a punishing
evil stranger, I can always
remember that here was a man
who was a worker and provider,
who learned the simple facts
in life and lived by them,
who held no pretense.

In other poems, we hear more than one speaker. For example, in "On a Night of Snow" we hear voices engaging in a *dialogue*, or a conversation between two people. Can you identify the two speakers in these lines from the poem?

I will bring you a saucer of milk like a marguerite,
So white and so smooth, so spherical and so sweet.
Stay with me, Cat. Outdoors the wild winds blow.

Mistress, there are portents abroad of magic and might,
And things that are yet to be done. Open the door!

The two speakers are the cat and its owner, and they have extremely different opinions on whether to go out or stay inside on a stormy winter night. The two speakers' words are written in different stanzas in order to help readers understand that a new speaker is talking in the second stanza. The first speaker, the cat's owner, is using gentle persuasion to convince the cat that inside by the fire is the place to stay. The second speaker, the cat, gives its reasons for wanting to enter the magic of the night and then commands that the door be opened. If you were one of the speakers in this poem, which one would you be?

EXERCISE ②

Reread "I'm Nobody! Who are you?" Then use what you have learned in this lesson to answer these questions:

1. Would you classify this poem as a dialogue or a monologue? Why?

2. In which stanza is it obvious that the speaker is talking to another person? Which words or phrases make this clear? In which stanza does the speaker seem to be thinking aloud and addressing no one in particular?

Now check your answers with your teacher. Review this part of the lesson if you don't understand why an answer was incorrect.

 WRITING ON YOUR OWN ②

In this lesson you learned about monologues and dialogues in poems. Now you will decide how to include a dialogue in the poem you will write. Follow these steps:

- Your poem should feature at least two characters. Look back at the outline of story events that you created in the previous writing exercise. At what points would a conversation between characters be likely? Make a list of possible situations for dialogues.
- Now look over your list and choose one of the possibilities. Divide a sheet of paper into as many columns as there are speakers in the conversation. In the first column, write what the first speaker might say in a conversation. In the second column, write what the second speaker would say, and so on.
- Save your dialogue ideas for the next writing assignments in this unit.

LESSON ③　SPEAKERS IN NARRATIVE POEMS

During the first half of the 20th century, Americans enjoyed the Golden Age of Radio. Every day, people would crowd around their radios to listen to programs that featured a variety of exciting stories. Radio stories were popular with listeners of all ages; people liked to invent their own mental pictures of the action as they listened to the storyteller, or narrator. The narrator's voice and way of speaking set the mood for the story and prepared listeners for the events that were about to happen.

When poets write *narrative poems*, or poems that tell a story, they understand the power that the narrator has over the story. A speaker who uses a casual, lighthearted tone can take the mystery out of the scariest ghost story. A speaker who speaks in a cold, informal tone can take the fun out of the most hilarious joke. That is why poets take care to develop speakers who match the story that they want to tell and the mood that they want to create.

"Molly Means" is the story of an evil witch who delights in casting spells over innocent neighbors. You can imagine this story being told late at night, after the lights have been turned off. Poet Margaret Walker has chosen a speaker who sounds as if he or she enjoys frightening listeners and uses a *dialect*, or particular way of speaking, that suggests the culture in which the story of Molly Means is set. These things add to the tale's authenticity:

> Old Molly Means was a hag and a witch;
> Chile of the devil, the dark, and sitch.
> Her heavy hair hung thick in ropes
> And her blazing eyes was black as pitch.
> Imp at three and wench at 'leben
> She counted her husbands to the number seben.
> 　　O Molly, Molly, Molly Means
> 　　There goes the ghost of Molly Means.

The unusual words, phrases, and dialect help you picture the storyteller and get you ready for a deliciously scary ghost story.

"The Highwayman" tells another kind of ghost story. In this poem, the speaker is more concerned with telling a dreamlike tale of love, danger, and death than with making readers scream in terror. For this reason, the speaker is more refined and uses language carefully and precisely in an old-fashioned style:

> He'd a French cocked-hat on his forehead, a bunch of
>   lace at his chin,
> A coat of the claret velvet, and breeches of brown
>   doeskin.
> They fitted with never a wrinkle. His boots were up
>   to the thigh.
> And he rode with a jeweled twinkle,
>   His pistol butts a-twinkle,
> His rapier hilt a-twinkle, under the jeweled sky.

The speaker tells the story with a noticeable rhythm, like the rhythm of a horse galloping on the "ribbon of moonlight over the purple moor." He or she repeats words ("marching—/Marching—marching—") and phrases ("Then look for me by moonlight/Watch for me by moonlight/I'll come to thee by moonlight, though hell should bar the way!") to suggest the insistent rhythm of the horse's hooves, bringing the highwayman back to the old inn.

In both poems, the speaker has been carefully chosen and painstakingly developed to ensure that the story has the greatest possible effect. When you read narrative poems, be sure to pay attention not only to the story but also to the speaker's role in telling it.

EXERCISE ③

Refer to "The Highwayman" and use what you have learned in this lesson to answer these questions:

1. The highwayman is actually a criminal who robs unsuspecting travelers, and the stable helper who turns him in is merely obeying the law. Compare the ways these two characters are described to find out which one the speaker admires more.

2. The speaker in "The Highwayman" tells the story from the third-person point of view. The third-person point of view may be *omniscient,* that is, able to report on the actions and thoughts of characters in different times and places. The third-person point of view also may be *limited,* that is, able to report on only one character's point of view. Which type of third-person point of view is used in "The Highwayman"? Give evidence from the poem to support your answer.

Now check your answers with your teacher. Review this part of the lesson if you don't understand why an answer was incorrect.

WRITING ON YOUR OWN ③

You already have written an outline for your narrative poem and decided on a speaker. Now follow these steps:

- Review the story outline and the speaker you chose for your poem. Now think about the mood you want to create in your poem. You may choose one of these moods or another one that matches the story you are telling: humorous, frightening, gentle, frantic, nervous, peaceful.
- Decide how the speaker could help create the mood within the first few lines of the poem. For example, if the mood were frightening as it is in "Molly Means," the speaker might

describe a frightening or weird sight using an attention-getting style of speech.

- Now write just the first stanza of your poem. If you'd like, you may imitate one of the patterns of regular rhythm and rhyme that you find in such poems as "Miniver Cheevy," "The Highwayman," or "Molly Means." Otherwise use an irregular, conversational style as is found in "The Runaway."

- Be sure that the topic that the speaker focuses on, the words he or she uses to describe it, and the way he or she speaks all help to create the mood and prepare your readers for the story to come. (You will write the rest of the poem in the next writing exercise.)

DISCUSSION GUIDES

1. How do you feel about poems written in dialect ? Do you enjoy trying to recreate the sound of the dialect as you read, or does the unusual spelling and phrasing confuse you and distract you from the meaning of the poem? Get together with a small group and read "Molly Means" aloud. Then discuss your answers to these questions.

2. In "On a Night of Snow," the cat insists on going outside to roam in the wild night. Some people don't let their cats roam outside because they don't want them to get hurt. Some communities even have laws forbidding cat owners to let their cats roam outside. Other cat lovers say that keeping a cat locked inside is unnatural and cruel. Where do you stand on this issue? Should cats be kept inside or allowed to roam neighborhoods freely? Present reasons for your opinion in a group discussion.

3. Carl Sandburg is sometimes said to be the poet of the common person because he often uses common, everyday language without obvious rhythm or rhyme. With a classmate, locate several other Sandburg poems and practice reading them aloud as you think they should be read. Then present them to the rest of the class in a Carl Sandburg poetry reading session.

WRITE A NARRATIVE POEM

In this unit you have focused on the speakers in various poems. Now you will write your own narrative poem that has a strong, well-developed speaker.

Follow these steps to write your poem. If you have questions about the writing process, refer to Using the Writing Process on page 232.

- Assemble and review the work you did for all the writing exercises in this unit: 1) lists of possible events for a story-poem; 2) a listing of major events and a paragraph explaining the speaker and why you chose him, her, or it; 3) a dialogue between two characters; 4) the first stanza of your narrative poem.

- Look over your list of major events for your story. Try to limit the number of events to no more than six. Any more might make your poem too complicated.

- List your characters and beside each one write a phrase or sentence that describes him, her, or it.

- Begin your poem with the stanza that you wrote for Writing on Your Own 3. Then write the rest of your poem, making sure that you match the style of the first stanza. Recall the mood that you wish to communicate and make sure your speaker's words and way of speaking help to create that mood. Include at least one dialogue, writing each character's words on a new line.

- Read your poem aloud and look for ways that you might make the order of events clearer and the characters more interesting. Also be sure that your speaker's voice remains consistent and strong throughout the poem.

- When you finish, go back and proofread your poem for spelling, grammar, and punctuation errors. Then make a final copy and save it in your writing portfolio.

Sensory Images and Concrete Language

INTRODUCTION

ABOUT THE LESSONS

Artists who paint portraits use all of their skills to reproduce the likeness of a person on canvas. Not only do they try to duplicate the details they can see—such as the shape of the eyes and the mouth—they also try to reflect the personality of the subject, perhaps by putting a certain expression in the eyes or capturing the subject's trademark smile. When you look at a particular portrait, you learn not only about the person's appearance, but to some extent, you also learn about his or her personality. Like artists, poets try to reproduce and recreate people, places, and moments, using words instead of paints and brushes.

The poets whose work is represented in this unit are experts at painting with words. Their poems are divided into two groups. The poems in Group 1 show the way poets use sensory details and concrete words to recreate a sight or a special moment. The poems in Group 2 examine how sensory images help to convey the mood of a poem.

 WRITING: DESCRIBING A PERSON OR PLACE

In this unit you will examine how poets develop images to support the mood of a poem. At the end of the unit you will write an original poem with striking images. Follow these steps to start you thinking about potential subjects for your poem:

- Think of people you know so well that you could describe them from memory. They may be friends, family members, schoolmates, or people from your neighborhood. Write each person's name on a list, and next to it write one sensory detail that you associate with that person.
- Now list places that you know well and feel strongly about. You might list a room in your home, your classroom, or any

other place where you spend a great deal of time. Next to each room, record one sensory detail that you associate with that place.

- Save your lists. You will use them again in later writing exercises.

ABOUT THIS POET	Robert Hayden (1913–1980) was born Asa Bundy Sheffey in Detroit, Michigan, but his name was legally changed at a later date by his foster parents. He earned his bachelor's degree from Wayne State University and his master's degree from the University of Michigan. During the 1930s, Hayden did extensive research on American history for the Federal Writers' Project in Detroit and focused especially on the African-American experience. At the University of Michigan, he became interested in the Civil War and eventually won the Hopwood Award for his series of poems about that period. Hayden became an English teacher at Fisk University, where he stayed for 23 years. He ended his teaching career after 11 more years at the University of Michigan. Although Hayden enjoyed teaching, he admitted that he was "a poet who teaches in order to earn a living so that he can write a poem or two now and then."

In 1966 Hayden published *Selected Poems*, which became an immediate success with critics. Over the next 10 years, he published several other volumes, assuring his place among respected American poets. In 1976 he was appointed as Consultant in Poetry to the Library of Congress, a position he held for two years.

Hayden's best-known poem, called "Middle Passage," tells the story of the 1839 mutiny of slaves led by Cinquez on the slave ship *Amistad*. While it is true that in many of his poems, Hayden writes about African Americans such as Nat Turner, Malcolm X, Harriet Tubman, and Frederick Douglass, in other poems he writes about purely personal thoughts and feelings.

Although Hayden was African American, he wished to be considered simply an American poet. His success in meeting his goal is reflected in the great number of awards and honors that were given to him by a variety of organizations, including the World Festival of Negro Arts, the National Institute of Arts and Letters, The Academy of American Poets, and the Michigan Arts Foundation.

AS YOU READ

As you read each poem in this unit, ask yourself the following questions:

- How does this poem appeal to my senses? Which images do I find most memorable?
- What is the mood of this poem? Why has the poet chosen these particular images to communicate the mood?

Petals

by Pat Mora

ABOUT THE SELECTION

Pat Mora (1942–   ) was born and raised in El Paso, Texas. She has written several volumes of poetry, as well as a collection of essays and a number of children's books. She works energetically to preserve the Mexican-American culture; one of her goals is to introduce Hispanic viewpoints to a wider audience. In the following poem, she writes about the thoughts and experiences of a Mexican street merchant. Note that the title of this poem is also, in effect, its first line. For more information about Pat Mora, see About This Poet in Unit 7.

have calloused her hands,
brightly colored crepe paper: turquoise,
yellow, magenta, which she shapes
into large blooms for bargain-hunting tourists
who see her flowers, her puppets, her baskets,
but not her—small, gray-haired woman
wearing a white apron, who hides behind
blossoms in her stall at the market,
who sits and remembers collecting wildflowers
as a girl, climbing rocky Mexican hills
to fill a straw hat with soft blooms
which she'd stroke gently, over and over again
with her smooth fingertips.

Cleaning the Well

by Paul Ruffin

ABOUT THE SELECTION

Paul Ruffin (1942–   ) is a poet and a teacher as well as the editor of the *Texas Review*. You can find examples of his poems in a number of magazines and other publications. This particular poem is taken from one of his collections of poetry called *Lighting the Furnace Pilot*. Notice how he appeals to more than one sense and uses exact words to set a mood in this poem.

Each spring there was the well to be cleaned.
On a day my grandfather would say,
"It's got to be done. Let's go." This time
I dropped bat and glove, submitted to the rope,
and he lowered me into the dark and cold
water of the well. The sun
slid off at a crazy cant[1] and I
was there, thirty feet down, waist deep
in icy water, grappling for whatever
was not pure and wet and cold.
The sky hovered like some pale moon
above, eclipsed by his heavy red face
bellowing down to me not to dally,
to feel deep and load the bucket.
My feet rasped against cold stone,
toes selecting unnatural shapes, curling
and gripping, raising them to my fingers,

---

[1] angle; tilt

then into the bucket and up to him:
a rubber ball, pine cones, leather glove,
beer can, fruit jars, an indefinable bone.
It was a time of fears: suppose he
should die or forget me, the rope break,
the water rise, a snake strike, the
bottom give way, the slick sides crumble?

The last bucket filled, my grandfather
assured, the rope loop dropped to me
and I was delivered by him who
sent me down, drawn slowly to sun
and sky and his fiercely grinning face.
"There was something else down there:
a cat or possum skeleton, but it
broke up, I couldn't pick it up."

He dropped his yellow hand on my head.
"There's always something down there
you can't quite get in your hands.
You'd know that if it wasn't your first
trip down. You'll know from now on."

"But what about the water?
Can we keep on drinking it?"

"You've drunk all that cat
you're likely to drink. Forget it
and don't tell the others. It's just
one more secret you got to live with."

It's Hot in the City

by Peter West

ABOUT THE SELECTION

If you've ever been in a big city on a hot summer day, you will surely recall some of the details and experiences that Peter West describes in the following poem. Try to pick out some of the words he uses that appeal to each of your senses.

White light glares on car rails, cobbles,
Swirling dust, and scraps of paper
Stirred by baked enamel autos.
Shirt-sleeved drivers, forearms upright
Sweat and swear and steer one-handed.
Sickly-sweet, warm, wafted smells—from
Joe's Place and the Lucky Garden—
Mingling, bring no invitation.

Lolling dogs droop in dead doorways.
Children seek the soiled and struggling
Patch of earthy grass between the
Bus stop and the supermarket;
Lining up to bow and gasp in
Turn at the delicious shock of
Water gushing from the fountain.

Damp, red men and moist, pale women
Feel the grilling sidewalks reach up,
Suck vitality through shoe soles
Down toward the earth's hot centre.
Old folk, wise, released from tension,
Rock, or fan themselves on porches
By front steps of teeming houses.

But
Nobody hurries.

Friday: and man flies, gasping
From what he has made
Out, off and away
To the cool wood,
The sweet turf
Or the limpid lake—
To breathe. . . .

It's HOT in the city.

Those Winter Sundays

by Robert Hayden

ABOUT THE SELECTION

Robert Hayden (1913–1980) was born and raised in Detroit, Michigan, and graduated from Wayne State University. For many years he taught English at Fisk University and the University of Michigan. In 1976 Hayden became the first African American to serve as poetry consultant to the Library of Congress. For more about Robert Hayden, see About This Poet at the beginning of this unit. Now look for the emotions that lie beneath the images in the following poem.

Sundays too my father got up early
and put his clothes on in the blueblack cold,
then with cracked hands that ached
from labor in the weekday weather made
banked fires blaze. No one ever thanked him.

I'd wake and hear the cold splintering, breaking.
When the rooms were warm, he'd call,
and slowly I would rise and dress,
fearing the chronic[1] angers of that house,

Speaking indifferently to him,
who had driven out the cold
and polished my good shoes as well.
What did I know, what did I know
of love's austere[2] and lonely offices?[3]

---

[1] always present; habitual

[2] severe; harsh

[3] duties

86

Living

by Denise Levertov

ABOUT THE SELECTION

Denise Levertov (1923–   ) was born in England and moved to the United States in 1948. She taught at a number of colleges before retiring from a full professorship at Tufts University. The topics in Levertov's poetry range from intensely personal to political, taking on issues such as poverty, war, and women's role in society. She prides herself on the precision of her writing. This precision is evident in the following poem.

The fire in leaf and grass
so green it seems
each summer the last summer.

The wind blowing, the leaves
shivering in the sun,
each day the last day.

A red salamander
so cold and so
easy to catch, dreamily

moves his delicate feet
and long tail. I hold
my hand open for him to go.

Each minute the last minute.

Oregon Winter

by Jeanne McGahey

ABOUT THE SELECTION

Most poems about winter describe ice, snow, cold winds, and sports like skiing and ice-skating. In the following poem, however, Jeanne McGahey describes a very different picture of winter, Oregon-style.

The rain begins. This is no summer rain,
Dropping the blotches of wet on the dusty road:
This rain is slow, without thunder or hurry:
There is plenty of time—there will be months of rain.
    Lost in the hills, the old gray farmhouses
Hump their backs against it, and smoke from their chimneys
Struggles through weighted air. The sky is sodden with water,
It sags against the hills, and the wild geese,
Wedge-flying, brush the heaviest cloud with their wings.
    The farmers move unhurried. The wood is in,
The hay has long been in, the barn lofts piled
Up to the high windows, dripping yellow straws.
There will be plenty of time now, time that will smell of fires,
And drying leather, and catalogues, and apple cores.
    The farmers clean their boots, and whittle, and drowse.

Sleeping in the Forest

by Mary Oliver

ABOUT THE SELECTION

Mary Oliver (1935–   ) was born in Cleveland, Ohio, and attended the Ohio State University and Vassar College. She has taught creative writing at Case Western Reserve University in Cleveland. Oliver won the Pulitzer Prize for poetry in 1984 for *American Primitive* and the National Book Award for *New and Selected Poems* in 1992. Many of her poems combine a sensitivity to the natural world around us and an awareness of our mortality. In this poem she makes us aware of the sensations that accompany a night in the forest.

I thought the earth
remembered me, she
took me back so tenderly, arranging
her dark skirts, her pockets
full of lichens and seeds. I slept
as never before, a stone
on the riverbed, nothing
between me and the white fire of the stars
but my thoughts, and they floated
light as moths among the branches
of the perfect trees. All night
I heard the small kingdoms breathing
around me, the insects, and the birds
who do their work in the darkness. All night
I rose and fell, as if in water, grappling
with a luminous doom. By morning
I had vanished at least a dozen times
into something better.

UNDERSTANDING THE POEMS

Record your answers to these questions in your personal literature notebook. Follow the directions for each group.

GROUP 1   Reread the poems in Group 1 to complete these sentences.

Reviewing the Selection

1. In "Petals" the street merchant's hands have become calloused by
   a. gathering flowers from Mexican hillsides.
   b. selling her flowers in a stall at the market place.
   c. making crepe-paper flowers.
   d. stroking the flowers she has gathered.

2. In "Cleaning the Well" the speaker is upset about leaving this object in the well:
   a. an animal skeleton.
   b. a rubber ball.
   c. his baseball glove.
   d. a water snake.

Interpreting the Selection

3. When the speaker in "It's Hot in the City" says that the smells from the restaurants "bring no invitation," he or she means that
   a. the food served at those restaurants is terrible.
   b. there are no signs posted to welcome diners.
   c. the restaurants have not sent out invitations.
   d. the smells do not make people hungry.

Recognizing How Words Are Used

4. When the speaker in "Cleaning the Well" says, "My feet rasped against the cold stone," the poet is appealing to the senses of
   a. sight and hearing.
   b. hearing and touch.
   c. touch and sight.
   d. smell and hearing.

Appreciating Poetry

5. In "It's Hot in the City" the overall impression that readers get about city life in the summer is
  a. beauty and sophistication.
  b. anger and frustration.
  c. heat, dirt, and discomfort.
  d. excitement and fun.

GROUP 2   Reread the poems in Group 2 to complete these sentences.

Reviewing the Selection

6. In "Those Winter Sundays" the father gets up early to
  a. start a fire in the fireplace or furnace.
  b. continue the argument he had started the day before.
  c. earn the gratitude of his family.
  d. have more time to talk to his family.

7. The setting for "Oregon Winter" is
  a. in a suburban area of homes and businesses.
  b. high up in the mountains.
  c. along the ocean coastline.
  d. in a rural location with farmhouses.

Interpreting the Selection

8. The following words from "Living" remind us to take a moment to treasure the beauty in our lives:
  a. the leaves/shivering in the sun.
  b. Each minute the last minute.
  c. I hold/my hand open for him to go.
  d. A red salamander/so cold and so/easy to catch.

Recognizing How Words Are Used

9. In "Sleeping in the Forest" thoughts are compared to
  a. birds working in the darkness.
  b. the earth's dark skirts.
  c. stones on the riverbed.
  d. moths floating among the branches.

Appreciating Poetry

10. The mood of "Those Winter Sundays" can be described as
a. excited.
b. regretful.
c. peaceful.
d. angry.

Now check your answers with your teacher. Study the questions you answered incorrectly. What types of questions were they? Talk with your teacher about ways to work on those skills.

Sensory Images and Concrete Language

If you watch the television news on New Year's Eve, you are likely to take a look back at the entire year in pictures. Your screen may be filled with a series of photographs—images briefly flashed on the screen to remind you of some of the year's important events. You need only see an image for a few seconds to remember the story attached to it and the emotions you felt when you saw it for the first time.

Poets understand the power of images to evoke feelings. For that reason they often use images in their poems to recreate experiences, impressions, and moods. Some poems are like photographs. They seem so real that you can almost reach out and touch the images described in them. Poets create this reality by using *sensory images*—words and phrases that appeal to your senses—and *concrete language*, words and phrases that describe things that can be experienced through the senses.

In the following lessons you will examine poems that use imagery effectively, and you will learn the following techniques that poets use to create memorable images:

- Poets include details that appeal to your senses and paint pictures with words.
- They include just the right imagery to help readers understand the mood of the poem.

LESSON 1   SENSORY IMAGES, CONCRETE LANGUAGE, AND EXACT WORDS

Suppose you went to a fancy restaurant for a special occasion and, unfortunately, your experience was less than satisfactory. If someone asked you for a review of the meal and the restaurant, you could say "Not so good." However, that reply would not be as helpful as a more specific description would be. For example, you could say that the hostess kept you waiting in a cold hall, the chairs were so soft you sank into them, the lettuce in the salad was limp and tasteless, the restaurant smelled like old cigarette smoke, the lights were harsh and hard to read by, the waiter was hurried and rude, and the music was way too loud. This review would be much more useful and informative. It would appeal to your listener's senses and would paint clear and specific images.

As you learned in Unit 1, details like the ones in your review are called sensory details because they describe things that can be experienced by the senses. A number of sensory details together can produce a sensory image—a clear picture of something that the senses can experience. Pat Mora makes use of sensory details to create the images in "Petals." Read the poem again, this time looking for details that appeal to your senses. You will find a number of visual details such as:

> brightly colored crepe paper: turquoise,
> yellow, magenta

and

> small, gray-haired woman
> wearing a white apron

You also will find these details that appeal to your sense of touch:

> remembers collecting wildflowers
> as a girl, climbing rocky Mexican hills
> to fill a straw hat with soft blooms
> which she'd stroke gently, over and over again.

Notice, also, the difference in the description of the street merchant's hands now—"calloused"—and her hands as a girl—"smooth fingertips." All of these details combine to produce a clear and sympathetic sensory image of the street merchant.

Experiences also can be recreated by the use of concrete language. When writers use concrete language, they call up an image in your mind by specifically mentioning something that you can see, smell, touch, hear, or taste. For example, *daisy, garbage can lid,* and *lemonade* are concrete words because they can be seen, smelled, heard, touched, and tasted. *Patriotism, faith,* and *honor,* however, are abstract words because they represent ideas, which cannot be experienced by the senses.

When you are trying to create a sensory image, concrete words are much more effective than abstract words. For example, notice how real the concrete words make the experience of the speaker in "Cleaning the Well":

> My feet rasped against cold stone,
> toes selecting unnatural shapes, curling
> and gripping, raising them to my fingers,
> then into the bucket and up to him:
> a rubber ball, pine cones, leather glove,
> beer can, fruit jars, an indefinable bone.

The speaker doesn't say that his or her feet just hit the sides of the well. Instead, they "rasped" against its "cold stone." These carefully chosen words help you understand that the walls of the well were cold, rough, scratchy, and unpleasant. Then later in the poem the speaker's grandfather is not just smiling, he is "fiercely grinning." The words that the poet uses are not vague or even adequate; they are perfect for communicating the images that he wants us to see in our minds.

EXERCISE ①

Reread "It's Hot in the City" by Peter West. Then use what you have learned in this lesson to answer these questions:

1. Select five sensory details from this poem and identify the sense that each one appeals to most. Try to include as many senses as possible in your answer.

2. Find at least three examples of concrete language in the poem. Remember that concrete words identify things that can be experienced by the senses.

3. Rephrase the following lines, this time without using exact, specific words. (In other words, make your rewording as dull and vague as possible.)

> White light glares on car rails, cobbles,
> Swirling dust, and scraps of paper
> Stirred by baked enamel autos.

> Damp, red men and moist, pale women
> Feel the grilling sidewalks reach up,
> Suck vitality through shoe soles
> Down toward the earth's hot centre.

Now check your answers with your teacher. Review this part of the lesson if you don't understand why an answer was incorrect.

 WRITING ON YOUR OWN ①

Earlier in this unit you listed people and places that you know well enough to describe in a poem. Now you will focus on one person or place. Follow these steps:

- Look over your lists of people and places. As you read each item on the lists, mark a few people and places that you see most clearly and feel most strongly about. For example, when you read about your garden, you may feel its peace or see your favorite flowers clearly. Then choose the one item—either a person or a place—that appeals to you most strongly.

- Now picture your chosen person or place. To focus on details that you associate with that person or place, divide a sheet of paper into five columns, one for each sense. In each column, list as many sensory details and concrete words as you can about your chosen person or place.

LESSON ② IMAGES AND MOOD

The *mood* of a piece of writing is the atmosphere or feeling it creates. A poet develops a mood in a number of ways, including carefully choosing images that support the mood. For example, the image of moonlight over a sleeping village might create a peaceful mood, while the image of fire engines racing through busy streets with sirens blaring probably creates a frantic, excited mood.

Jeanne McGahey, who wrote "Oregon Winter," wants to create a damp, heavy, slow-moving mood as she describes the onset of winter in the rainy Northwest. Read these lines from her poem and notice how the images support the mood:

> There is plenty of time—there will be months of rain.
>   Lost in the hills, the old gray farmhouses
> Hump their backs against it, and smoke from their
>   chimneys
> Struggles through weighted air. The sky is sodden
>   with water,
> It sags against the hills, and the wild geese,
> Wedge-flying, brush the heaviest cloud with their wings.

The images suggest the heavy, resigned mood that can come from experiencing a long rainy period, rather than the fleeting excitement that can come from a thunderstorm. In addition to choosing these images, McGahey uses words and phrases that help contribute to the poem's mood, for example: "hump their backs against it," "Struggles through weighted air," and "sodden with water." The *connotations* of these words—that is, the feelings the words give you beyond their *denotations*, or dictionary meanings—work together with the images to create the mood.

Contrast the mood of "Oregon Winter" with the one that Denise Levertov creates in "Living." The poem bristles with excitement and delight as the speaker celebrates nature, painfully aware that it is both beautiful and temporary. Notice how the feelings that the images in these lines create seem somehow more intense than those in "Oregon Winter":

> The fire in leaf and grass
> so green it seems
> each summer the last summer.
>
> The wind blowing, the leaves
> shivering in the sun,
> each day the last day.

The mood of "Those Winter Sundays" is just as intense as that of "Living." In this poem Robert Hayden surprises us with an unusual view of family life. Popular images of families are usually warm—firesides, hot meals, snuggling under warm quilts. However in "Those Winter Sundays," the images combine to convey the emotional coldness of the speaker's home, as in these lines from the poem:

> Sundays too my father got up early
> and put his clothes on in the blueblack cold, . . .
>
> I'd wake and hear the cold splintering, breaking. . . .
>
> Speaking indifferently to him,
> who had driven out the cold . . .

In this short poem the word *cold* is used three times. Even though the father has worked to make the rooms warm, the overall impression is one of uncomfortable coldness, both physical and emotional. Note how the poet has extended the feeling of coldness from being sensed only by touch to also being sensed by sight ("blueblack cold") and hearing ("hear the cold splintering, breaking"). This technique of combining images that relate to more than one sense intensifies and extends the images to help communicate the mood of the poem.

EXERCISE ②

Reread "Sleeping in the Forest." Then use what you have learned in this lesson to answer these questions:

1. How would you describe the mood of this poem? Which images support that mood?

2. The speaker describes his or her thoughts as "light as moths among the branches/of the perfect trees." Why is this simile more effective in supporting the mood of the poem than one such as "light as confetti" or "light as ashes"?

Now check your answers with your teacher. Review this part of the lesson if you don't understand why an answer was incorrect.

WRITING ON YOUR OWN ②

In this lesson you have seen how poets communicate moods through their use of precise images. Now you will focus on the images and mood of your own poem. Follow these steps:

• For each of the following moods, think of at least three images that would help to develop it. (You may want to work with a partner.) Divide a sheet of paper into four sections to record your ideas.

nervous   peaceful   sorrowful   weird or spooky

* Now think of a mood that was not listed above and on a new sheet of paper, list images that would help to develop it.
* Choose one of the five moods and write a short poem about it, beginning with the sentence stem "_____ is. . . ." Fill in the blank with the mood you have chosen, and complete the sentence with at least four different images. Here is an example: Nervous is seeing Mrs. Johnson at the front of the room, holding a folder with our math tests in it.

DISCUSSION GUIDES

1. In "Cleaning the Well" the speaker uses some vivid details to describe a distasteful chore. All of us have chores to do that are not to our liking. Think of the chore you dislike the most and list details about it that would help readers understand your feelings. Be sure to use sensory details and concrete words. Then share your list with your classmates and listen to some of their lists. Together, decide which jobs sound the worst, based on the images and details you have all listed.

2. Poet Peter West paints a vivid picture of a summer day in the city by appealing to readers' senses of sight, smell, hearing, and touch. Think about what someone might see, hear, smell, feel, and taste on a summer day in your city or town. Then fill out a web, or cluster map, like the one below.

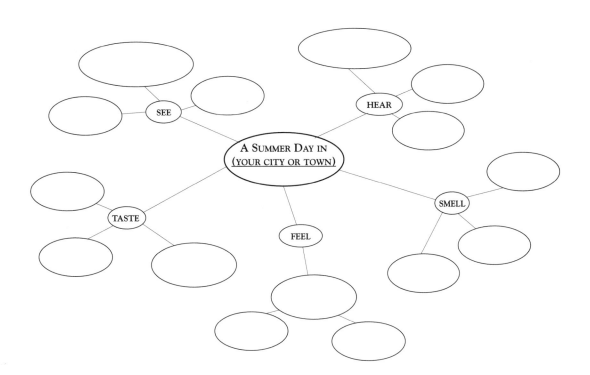

3. With a small group of classmates, choose four of the poems from this unit that you enjoy most and prepare an oral reading of them. Decide if one group member will read an entire poem or if you will switch readers for different lines or stanzas. Practice reading the poems aloud several times, and then tape your readings (either audio or video). Later, play your tape for the rest of the class and then watch or listen to theirs. You may want to keep track of which poems were chosen by more than one group and then discuss why those poems were your class's favorites.

WRITE A POEM WITH SENSORY IMAGES

In this unit you have focused on imagery in poems and have learned how images work together to help create a poem's mood. Now you will write an original poem using what you have learned.

Follow these steps to write your poem. If you have questions about the writing process, refer to Using the Writing Process on page 232.

- Assemble and review the work you did for all the writing exercises in this unit: 1) lists of people and places and associated sensory details, 2) sensory details and concrete words associated with one chosen person or place, 3) a list of images associated with certain moods and a short poem using some of those images.
- Look at your list of sensory details that describe a particular person or place. If you still wish to write your poem about that person or place, keep that list available. If you wish to change your person or place, do so now. Then make another list of sensory details for your new subject.
- Make a tentative decision about the mood of your poem before you begin, so you can keep it in mind as you write. However, don't be surprised if this mood changes after you begin to write.
- Write your poem. Use as many sensory details and concrete words as possible to help your readers see, hear, smell, taste, and share your experience. Be sure that each image you include helps to convey your chosen mood.
- Ask a classmate to read your poem and tell you what emotions it made him or her feel. If the mood is not clear enough, revise your poem until you feel that it conveys your chosen mood.
- Proofread your poem for spelling and grammar errors. Then make a final copy and save it in your writing portfolio.

Rhythm, Rhyme, and Repetition

INTRODUCTION

ABOUT THE LESSONS

The lessons in this unit explore the rhythm, rhyme, and repetition of sounds in poetry. Some of the sounds in a poem are very easy to recognize. For example, a steady rhythm and lines that end in rhymes are easy to read and hear. Other sounds, however, are more subtle and are not as easy to recognize. Using the poems in this unit, you will look at some of the ways in which poets use sound to give their words and ideas meaning.

WRITING: PREPARING TO WRITE POEMS

Throughout this unit you will see how different poets use sounds to create different effects. You also will work with a partner to develop techniques for using sounds in your own writing. At the end of the unit you and your partner will produce a small collection of poems that demonstrate your abilities. Begin thinking about topics for your poems by following these steps:

- For your poetry collection, you and your partner will need to produce four short poems about a single theme. For example, your poems could be about four types of weather—such as wind, rain, snow, and hail; four different mealtimes—such as breakfast, lunch, dinner, and snacktime; the four seasons; or four different colors, hobbies, or sports.

  Work with your partner to make a list of at least six themes that you could write about. (Feel free to use some of the preceding suggestions.) Then for each theme, list four related ideas that could be the topics of the four poems.
- Next, choose one of the themes, such as the seasons. Label four separate sheets of paper with its four related topics— winter, spring, summer, and autumn. By yourself or with your writing partner, brainstorm words or phrases that you associ-

ate with each topic. For autumn, for example, you might list words or phrases such as *cool weather, jackets, back-to-school, raking leaves, pumpkins,* and *football.* Also list comparisons that bring out some aspect of the topic—for example "the leaves are fiery jewels that sparkle in the trees."

- Repeat this procedure with at least one more theme. As you and your partner work through this unit, keep adding to your lists as more ideas come to you.
- Keep your work in your writing portfolio. You will use it again.

ABOUT THIS POET

Robert Frost (1874–1963), the most popular poet of his time, won the Pulitzer Prize for poetry in 1924, 1931, 1937, and 1943. He also was awarded a Congressional Medal on his 88th birthday, in recognition of the effect of his poetry on "the culture of the United States and the philosophy of the world."

Although he was born in San Francisco, Frost is identified with New England, the setting for almost all of his poems. His family moved back to its New England home in 1885, and he spent most of the rest of his life in the area. He briefly attended college at Dartmouth and Harvard and married in 1897.

As a young man Frost worked in New England as a farmer, an editor, and a teacher. During those years he also was writing poetry. Although some of his poems were published in magazines, he did not receive much recognition. In 1912 he moved his family to England, where he hoped to devote full time to his writing. While in England he met such important poets as William Butler Yeats and Ezra Pound. Frost's first two books of poems, *A Boy's Will* and *North of Boston*, were published in England and won favorable reviews. Having succeeded in England, Frost returned to the United States in 1915 as a famous poet. He spent the rest of his life back in the States, writing and lecturing.

In most of his poems Frost writes about the scenes and

people of New England in plain language, usually using traditional rhyming verse. His poetry appears simple but has many layers of meaning. To Frost, the nature that he describes so gracefully can be both beautiful and threatening. His poems suggest that people gain happiness by working hard for it. A few of his most popular poems are "The Mending Wall," "Stopping by Woods on a Snowy Evening," and "Death of the Hired Man." The last of his poetry collections was published in 1962.

AS YOU READ

As you read each poem in this unit, ask yourself the following questions:

- Does this poem have a rhythmic pattern or does it sound more like a conversation?
- Are there any rhyming words in this poem?
- Are any sounds, words, phrases, or lines repeated in this poem? If so, why might the poet have used them more than once?

How They Brought the Good News from Ghent to Aix

by Robert Browning

ABOUT THE SELECTION

Although Robert Browning (1812–1889) was one of the most critically acclaimed poets of England's Victorian Age, he was not recognized as a great poet until late in his life. Browning's work reflects his vigor, optimism, and faith in humanity. In 1846 he married Elizabeth Barrett, also a poet, and they moved to Florence, Italy. After Elizabeth died in 1861, Browning returned to England. There his poetry was so well received that when he died, he was buried with honor in Westminster Abbey, a church in London in which English kings and queens and other famous people are buried.

"How They Brought the Good News from Ghent to Aix" is set in the early 17th century during warfare between the Dutch states and Spain. However, the event it describes was invented by Browning. The poet never tells what the good news in the title is; he is concerned only with presenting the excitement of the speaker's journey on the noble horse, Roland.

I sprang to the stirrup, and Joris, and he;
I galloped, Dirck galloped, we galloped all three;
"Good speed!" cried the watch, as the gate bolts undrew,
"Speed!" echoed the wall to us galloping through;
Behind shut the postern,[1] the lights sank to rest,
And into the midnight we galloped abreast.

---

[1] a small rear gate, as in a fort or castle

Not a word to each other; we kept the great pace
Neck by neck, stride by stride, never changing our place;
I turned in my saddle and made its girths[2] tight,
Then shortened each stirrup, and set the pique right,
Rebuckled the cheek-strap, chained slacker the bit,[3]
Nor galloped less steadily Roland a whit.

'Twas moonset at starting; but while we drew near
Lokeren, the cocks crew and twilight dawned clear;
At Boom, a great yellow star came out to see;
At Düffeld, 'twas morning as plain as could be;
And from Mecheln church-steeple we heard the half-chime,
So, Joris broke silence with, "Yet there is time!"

At Aershot, up leaped of a sudden the sun,
And against him the cattle stood black every one,
To stare thro' the mist at us galloping past,
And I saw my stout galloper Roland at last,
With resolute shoulders, each butting away
The haze, as some bluff river headland its spray:

And his low head and crest, just one sharp ear bent back
For my voice, and the other pricked out on his track;
And one eye's black intelligence,—ever that glance
O'er its white edge at me, his own master askance![4]
And the thick heavy spume-flakes which aye and anon
His fierce lips shook upwards in galloping on.

By Hasselt, Dirck groaned; and cried Joris, "Stay spur!
Your Roos galloped bravely, the fault's not in her,
We'll remember at Aix"—for one heard the quick wheeze
Of her chest, saw the stretched neck and staggering knees,

---

[2] straps around a horse that hold a saddle in place

[3] *pique, cheek-strap,* and *bit* are all items in the gear used on a horse

[4] with a sideways glance

And sunk tail, and horrible heave of the flank,
As down on her haunches she shuddered and sank.

So, we were left galloping, Joris and I,
Past Looz and past Tongres, no cloud in the sky;
The broad sun above laughed a pitiless laugh,
'Neath our feet broke the brittle bright stubble like chaff;
Till over by Dalhem a dome-spire sprang white,
And "Gallop," gasped Joris, "for Aix is in sight!"

"How they'll greet us!"—and all in a moment his roan
Rolled neck and croup over, lay dead as a stone;
And there was my Roland to bear the whole weight
Of the news which alone could save Aix from her fate,
With his nostrils like pits full of blood to the brim,
And with circles of red for his eye-sockets' rim.

Then I cast loose my buffcoat, each holster let fall,
Shook off both my jack-boots, let go belt and all,
Stood up in the stirrup, leaned, patted his ear,
Called my Roland his pet-name, my horse without peer;
Clapped my hands, laughed and sang, any noise, bad or good
Till at length into Aix Roland galloped and stood.

And all I remember is—friends flocking round
As I sat with his head 'twixt my knees on the ground;
And no voice but was praising this Roland of mine,
As I poured down his throat our last measure of wine,
Which (the burgesses voted by common consent)
Was no more than his due who brought good news from Ghent.

The Yarn of the *Nancy Bell*

by Sir William Schwenck Gilbert

ABOUT THE SELECTION

Sir William Schwenck Gilbert (1836–1911) was a lawyer, a writer, and most notably, half of Gilbert and Sullivan, the most famous writing team in comic opera. Gilbert wrote the dialogue and song lyrics for such famous light operas as *H.M.S. Pinafore, The Mikado,* and *The Pirates of Penzance,* and Arthur Sullivan composed the music. Gilbert also directed the first productions of the famous team's works. Gilbert submitted "The Yarn of the *Nancy Bell,*" one of his earliest humorous ballads (story poems), to a magazine before he gained fame. The magazine decided it was too grisly to print.

'Twas on the shores that round our coast
    From Deal to Ramsgate span,
That I found alone on a piece of stone
    An elderly naval man.

His hair was weedy, his beard was long,
    And weedy and long was he,
And I heard this wight[1] on the shore recite
    In a singular minor key:

"Oh, I am a cook and a captain bold,
    And the mate of the *Nancy* brig,[2]
And a bo'sun[3] tight,[4] and a midshipmite,[5]
    And the crew of the captain's gig."[6]

---

[1] creature

[2] two-masted sailing ship

And he shook his fists, and he tore his hair,
 Till I really felt afraid,
For I couldn't help thinking the man had been drinking,
 And so I simply said:

"Oh elderly man, it's little I know
 Of the duties of men of the sea,
And I'll eat my hand if I understand
 However you can be

At once a cook, and a captain bold,
 And the mate of the *Nancy* brig,
And a bo'sun tight, and a midshipmite,
 And the crew of the captain's gig."

Then he gave a hitch to his trousers, which
 Is a trick all seamen larn,
And having got rid of a thumping quid,[7]
 He spun this painful yarn:

"'Twas in the good ship *Nancy Bell*
 That we sailed to the Indian Sea,
And there on a reef we came to grief,
 Which has often occurred to me.

And pretty nigh all the crew was drowned
 (There was seventy-seven o'soul),
And only ten of the *Nancy*'s men
 Said "Here!" to the muster-roll.[8]

---

[3] short for *boatswain,* an officer on a ship

[4] neat and trim in appearance

[5] dialect for *midshipmate,* a crew member

[6] long, light ship's boat, usually kept for the use of the captain

[7] cut of chewing tobacco

[8] list of members in a group used in calling attendance

There was me and the cook and the captain bold,
    And the mate of the *Nancy* brig,
And the bo'sun tight, and a midshipmite,
    And the crew of the captain's gig.

For a month we'd neither wittles[9] nor drink,
    Till a-hungry we did feel,
So we drawed a lot, and, accordin' shot
    The captain for our meal.

The next lot fell to the *Nancy*'s mate,
    And a delicate dish he made;
Then our appetite with the midshipmite
    We seven survivors stayed.

And then we murdered the bo'sun tight,
    And he much resembled the pig;
Then we wittled free, did the cook and me,
    On the crew of the captain's gig.

Then only the cook and me was left,
    And the delicate question, "Which
Of us two goes to the kettle?" arose,
    And we argued it out as sich.

For I loved that cook as a brother, I did,
    And the cook he worshiped me;
But we'd both be blowed if we'd either be stowed
    In the other chap's hold, you see.

"I'll be eat if you dines off me," says Tom;
    "Yes, that" says I "you'll be—"
"I'm boiled if I die, my friend," quoth I;
    And "Exactly so," quoth he.

---

[9] dialect for *vittles*, or food supplies

Says he, "Dear James, to murder me
    Were a foolish thing to do,
For don't you see that you can't cook *me*,
    While I can—and will—cook *you*!"

So he boils the water, and takes the salt
    And the pepper in portions true
(Which he never forgot) and some chopped shallot,
    And some sage and parsley too.

"Come here," says he, with a proper pride
    Which his smiling features tell,
"'Twill soothing be if I let you see
    How extremely nice you'll smell."

And he stirred it round and round and round,
    And he sniffed at the foaming froth;
When I ups with his heels, and smothers his squeals
    In the scum of the boiling broth.

And I eat that cook in a week or less,
    And—as I eating be
The last of his chops, why, I almost drops,
    For a wessel in sight I see!
    ....

And I never larf, and I never smile,
    And I never lark nor play,
But sit and croak, a single joke
    I have—which is to say:

"Oh, I am a cook and a captain bold,
    And the mate of the *Nancy* brig,
And a bo'sun tight, and a midshipmite,
    And the crew of the captain's gig!"

The Sprinters

by Lillian Morrison

ABOUT THE SELECTION

Lillian Morrison (1917–   ) is a well-known poet who also worked for 40 years as a librarian for the New York Public Library. She was born in Jersey City, New Jersey, graduated from Rutgers University, and earned her degree in library science at Columbia. She has had seven collections of her own poetry published and has compiled another seven books of poetry by other poets, mostly for children and young adults. She has written many poems that combine two of her loves: the rhythms of poetry and the rhythmic movements of sports. "The Sprinters" is one of those poems.

The gun explodes them.
Pummeling,[1] pistoning[2] they fly
In time's face.
A go at the limit,
A terrible try
To smash the ticking glass,
Outpace the beat
That runs, that streaks away
Tireless, and faster than they.

Beside ourselves

---

[1] beating, as with fists

[2] moving back and forth with regularity, as would a piston in an engine

(It is for us they run!)
We shout and pound the stands
For one to win,
Loving him, whose hard
Grace-driven stride
Most mocks the clock
And almost breaks the bands
Which lock us in.

A Time to Talk

by Robert Frost

ABOUT THE SELECTION

Robert Frost (1874–1963) was a farmer in New England for about 10 years before establishing his fame as a poet. Although he was not very successful as a farmer, his experiences during this time gave him much valuable material for his poems. In "A Time to Talk," readers can imagine hearing from farmer Frost. For more information about Frost, see About This Poet at the beginning of this unit.

When a friend calls to me from the road
And slows his horse to a meaning[1] walk,
I don't stand still and look around
Over all the hills I haven't hoed,
And shout from where I am, "What is it?"
No, not as there is a time to talk.
I thrust my hoe in the mellow ground,
Blade-end up and five feet tall,
And plod: I go up to the stone wall
For a friendly visit.

---

[1] meaningful

Jenny Kissed Me

by Leigh Hunt

ABOUT THE SELECTION

Leigh Hunt (1784–1859) was a friend of many of the great English poets of his time. In addition to writing poetry, he wrote essays and political articles and was the editor of several magazines. At one point his radical political opinions landed him in jail for a three-year period, but he continued to write in spite of his imprisonment. He supported such poets as John Keats and Percy Shelley before they were widely accepted. Today his most famous poems include "Abou Ben Adhem" and the one below, "Jenny Kissed Me."

Jenny kissed me when we met,
    Jumping from the chair she sat in.
Time, you thief, who love to get
    Sweets into your list, put that in.
Say I'm weary, say I'm sad;
    Say that health and wealth have missed me;
Say I'm growing old, but add—
    Jenny kissed me!

The Kiss

by Sara Teasdale

ABOUT THE SELECTION

Sara Teasdale (1884–1933) was one of the most popular poets of the early twentieth century. She was born in St. Louis, Missouri, and was educated at home. She traveled widely in Europe and the Near East before settling in New York City and devoting herself to writing poetry. Frequently ill, she preferred to live withdrawn from society. Her poems express simple but strong emotions and were so popular that one of her collections, *Love Songs* (published 1917), went through five editions in one year. In recognition of this event, she was awarded the first Pulitzer Prize for poetry in 1918. Even though "The Kiss" is a relatively light poem, it indicates her desire for deep feeling.

I hoped that he would love me,
    And he has kissed my mouth,
But I am like a stricken[1] bird
    That cannot reach the south.

For though I know he loves me,
    Tonight my heart is sad;
His kiss was not so wonderful
    As all the dreams I had.

---

[1] wounded

Song

by Katherine Philips

| ABOUT THE SELECTION | The phrasing and word choice of this short poem by Katherine Philips (1631–1664) reflect the fact that this English poet died over 300 years ago. However, the poem's message may remind you of the familiar modern message of Murphy's Law: If anything *can* go wrong, it will. |

'Tis true our life is but a long dis-ease,
Made up of real pain and seeming ease.
You stars, who these entangled fortunes give,
    O tell me why
    It is so hard to die,
    Yet such a task to live!

If with some pleasure we our griefs betray,
It costs us dearer than it can repay.
For time or fortune[1] all things so devours,
    Our hopes are crossed,
    Or else the object lost,
    Ere[2] we can call it ours.

---

[1] chance; luck

[2] before

Nothing Gold Can Stay

by Robert Frost

ABOUT THE SELECTION

The poems of Robert Frost (1874–1963), winner of four Pulitzer Prizes for poetry, are known for being deceptively simple. "Nothing Gold Can Stay" illustrates that quality. For more information about Frost, see About This Poet at the beginning of this unit.

Nature's first green is gold,
Her hardest hue[1] to hold.
Her early leaf's a flower,
But only so an hour.
Then leaf subsides[2] to leaf.
So Eden sank to grief,
So dawn goes down to day.
Nothing gold can stay.

---

[1] shade of a color

[2] sinks or settles down

Fireworks

by Babette Deutsch

ABOUT THE SELECTION

Babette Deutsch (1895–1982) was a prize-winning writer of poetry, fiction, and nonfiction for both children and adults. She also was noted for her many translations of Russian literature into English. Her first poetry collection was published in 1919; *The Collected Poems of Babette Deutsch* came out 50 years later, in 1969. Many of her poems express her reactions to paintings, sculpture, music, or other writers' works. "Fireworks," however, describes a less permanent form of art.

Not guns, not thunder, but a flutter of clouded drums
That announce a fiesta: abruptly, fiery needles
Circumscribe[1] on the night boundless chrysanthemums.
Softly, they break apart, they flake away, where
Darkness, on a svelte[2] hiss, swallows them.
Delicate brilliance: a bellflower opens, fades,
In a sprinkle of falling stars.
Night absorbs them
With the sponge of her silence.

---

[1] draw a line around

[2] graceful

Full Fathom Five

by William Shakespeare

ABOUT THE SELECTION

William Shakespeare (1564-1616) is widely considered the greatest playwright of all time and the finest poet to use the English language. He was born, educated, and married in Stratford-upon-Avon, a small town in England. He then became an actor and playwright in London, and a member of a popular company of actors that often performed for royalty. Around 1608, Shakespeare retired to Stratford. He is best known for his plays, including comedies, tragedies, and historical plays, written mostly in verse. In the magical comedy *The Tempest,* the spirit Ariel sings the song "Full Fathom Five" to a young man who mistakenly believes his father has drowned in a shipwreck. Ariel suggests that even out of death comes beauty.

Full fathom[1] five thy father lies;
Of his bones are coral made;
Those are pearls that were his eyes;
Nothing of him that doth[2] fade
But doth suffer a sea-change
Into something rich and strange.
Sea-nymphs[3] hourly ring his knell:[4]
Ding-dong.
Hark! now I hear them, ding-dong, bell.

---

[1] a unit of length equal to 6 feet, used primarily in measuring depths of bodies of water

[2] an old-fashioned way of saying *does*

[3] in myth, a beautiful maiden who represents a feature of nature, such as the rivers or seas

[4] the sound of a bell ringing slowly and solemnly, as for a funeral

UNDERSTANDING THE POEMS

Record your answers to these questions in your personal literature notebook. Follow the directions for each group.

GROUP 1   Reread the poems in Group 1 to complete these sentences.

Reviewing the Selection

1. The good news mentioned in the poem "How They Brought the Good News from Ghent to Aix" is
   a. about who won a horse race.
   b. the results of a recent battle.
   c. about who won a war long ago.
   d. never explained in the poem.

2. The elderly naval man in "The Yarn of the *Nancy Bell*" admits that he
   a. is a deserter from the Navy.
   b. killed and ate his shipmates.
   c. caused the wreck of his ship.
   d. led a mutiny and took over his ship.

Interpreting the Selection

3. "The Sprinters" is *most* concerned with the feelings of
   a. the runners themselves.
   b. the officials who start and judge the race.
   c. the spectators at the race.
   d. the coaches who trained the runners.

Recognizing How Words Are Used

4. When "The Sprinters" says that the gun explodes the runners it means that the
   a. runners are shot by the gun.
   b. gun is so loud that it sounds like an explosion.
   c. runners are shot out of the gun.
   d. sound of the gun makes the runners burst into action.

Appreciating Poetry

5. "The Yarn of the *Nancy Bell*" best illustrates the power of poetry to

a. make important philosophical statements.

b. make us laugh.

c. capture sensory experiences through well-chosen details.

d. express personal feelings.

GROUP 2   Reread the poems in Group 2 to complete these sentences.

Reviewing the Selection

6. The poem in this group that is obviously set on a farm is

a. "A Time to Talk."

b. "Jenny Kissed Me."

c. "The Kiss."

d. "Song."

Interpreting the Selection

7. In "Jenny Kissed Me" the speaker directs his comments to Time because

a. he is hallucinating and thinks he sees time as a person.

b. he wants this experience to be recalled in a future time.

c. "Time" is the name of a person who is a thief.

d. this is a happy time for him.

8. The attitude of the speaker in "A Time to Talk" is

a. frustration at the interruption.

b. appreciation for friendship.

c. relief and gratitude for the break from work.

d. eager curiosity about local gossip.

Recognizing How Words Are Used

9. In "Song" the phrase "if with some pleasure we our griefs betray" means

a. if we take pleasure in ignoring our griefs.

b. if our griefs take pleasure in ignoring us.

c. if our pleasure ignores us by betraying our griefs.

d. all of the above.

Appreciating Poetry

10. The poet's purpose in writing "The Kiss" is to

    a. tell an exciting story.

    b. influence readers to take a particular action.

    c. express the emotion of joy.

    d. express the emotion of disappointment.

GROUP 3

Reread the poems in Group 3 to complete these sentences.

Reviewing the
Selection

11. "Full Fathom Five" describes

    a. an underwater statue.

    b. what happens to a drowned body.

    c. the sound of a church bell.

    d. a storm at sea.

12. The poem "Fireworks" describes the

    a. colors and shapes of fireworks.

    b. colors and sounds of fireworks.

    c. sounds and shapes of fireworks.

    d. colors and numbers of fireworks.

Interpreting the
Selection

13. The message of "Nothing Gold Can Stay" is that

    a. everyone spends money too fast.

    b. intense feelings and events do not last long.

    c. autumn leaves fall quickly.

    d. we don't recognize good things until they're gone.

Recognizing How
Words Are Used

14. In "Fireworks" the sound of the first fireworks is described as "a *flutter* of clouded drums." The word *flutter* brings to mind a bird rapidly flapping its wings. It is used to suggest that

    a. the fireworks exploding sound like birds flapping their wings.

    b. the fireworks look like drums as they spread out over the sky.

    c. the fireworks look like clouds as they shoot into the sky.

    d. that the fireworks will chase any night birds away.

Appreciating Poetry   **15.** The theme of "Nothing Gold Can Stay" is best suggested by the words

a. gold, hue, hour.

b. leaf, flower, day.

c. subsides, sank, goes down.

d. green, gold, dawn.

Now check your answers with your teacher. Study the questions you answered incorrectly. What types of questions were they? Talk with your teacher about ways to work on those skills.

Rhythm, Rhyme, and Repetition

The earliest poems were not written down. They were made up in a poet's mind and recited to an audience. The audience would memorize the poems they liked and then turn around and recite them to others. Today, because it is so easy to record poems in writing or on tape, we rarely exercise our memories as past generations did. When we do want to memorize a poem, however, we rely on the same techniques that those first audiences did.

One technique for remembering a poem is to pay attention to how it sounds. For example, if we know that all the lines in a poem have the same number of syllables, we can count syllables mentally and tell if we forgot some words. If we know that several words in a phrase begin with the same sound, it is easier to remember the words and the phrase. If we know that there is a certain rhythm to the words and a particular pattern of rhyme at the ends of lines, we have ways to remember the rest of a poem. Even without considering the meaning of the poem, we can see there is importance to its sound alone. When we also recognize that the sound of a poem adds to its meaning, we gain an even greater appreciation for the poem.

The lessons in this unit will discuss some of the sounds in a poem and how those sounds affect the poem. The lessons also will discuss some of the techniques poets use to create certain sounds in poems:

- Poets can create patterns of accented and unaccented syllables that stress selected words and reinforce particular feelings.
- Poets can arrange rhyming words in selected patterns.
- Poets can repeat selected sounds, words, and phrases to suggest or emphasize particular words, feelings, and ideas.

LESSON 1

RHYTHM

Try to imagine a song in which every word is sung on the same note, with the same amount of emphasis, at the same speed, and for the same length of time as every other word. That's one song that would never be very popular. What makes a song popular is not only its words but its variation of sounds—its pattern of high and low notes, the differences in how long those notes are held, the changes in loudness and softness. Even in a rap tune that has little change in pitch, there is considerable change in the *rhythm*, or patterns of beats, and also in the speeds at which the rapper delivers his or her words. Our ears are pleased by the variations and patterns of sound. In the same way, much of the pleasure of reading a poem comes from its effect on our ears.

Notice, for example, how much fun it is to say and hear the rhythm of the words in "How They Brought the Good News from Ghent to Aix." Below, the syllables of the first four lines are marked to show a natural way to read them. Slanted lines (/) indicate which syllables should be stressed. Curved lines (∪) indicate which syllables are unstressed.

> ∪ /   ∪ ∪ / ∪ ∪ / ∪ ∪ /
> I sprang to the stirrup, and Joris, and he;
> ∪ / ∪   ∪   / ∪ ∪ / ∪ ∪   /
> I galloped, Dirck galloped, we galloped all three;
>   ∪   /   ∪ ∪   / ∪ ∪ / ∪   ∪ /
> "Good speed!" cried the watch, as the gate bolts undrew,
>   ∪   / ∪ ∪   / ∪ ∪ / ∪ ∪   /
> "Speed!" echoed the wall to us galloping through;

As you read this poem—even when you read it silently—you cannot avoid hearing the sound of the horses galloping. Not every poem has such a clear, strong pattern of beats. Different people may even read the lines of a single poem in different ways. But what is important is that in most poems readers are aware of alternating stresses that form rhythms, and these rhythms may recur throughout the poem.

Some poems are written in what is called *free verse*. Such poems sound like casual conversation, with no particular rhythmic patterns. Others follow a single strict pattern of beats from start to finish. The majority of poems lie between these two extremes. They alternate between two or three patterns or allow minor variations on only one or two patterns.

When you try to figure out the rhythm of a particular poem, you will need to read and analyze several lines to see what pattern or patterns occur most often. Where there are variations, you often will discover that the poet intentionally changed the rhythm for a special effect or simply to call attention to the phrase with the variation. Look, for example, at "The Yarn of the *Nancy Bell*." Here is the first stanza, with the stressed and unstressed syllables marked. How many stressed syllables are in each line? Are all lines the same, or is there a pattern in their variations? Analyze the second stanza on your own to discover whether or not the following pattern is unique to the first stanza.

> ∪ / ∪ / ∪ / ∪ /
> 'Twas on the shores that round our coast
> ∪ / ∪ / ∪ /
> From Deal to Ramsgate span,
> ∪∪ / ∪ / ∪∪ / ∪ /
> That I found alone on a piece of stone
> ∪ /∪ ∪ /∪ /
> An elderly naval man.

A comparison of the first stanza with others in the poem shows that every stanza has four stressed syllables in the first and third lines, and three in the second and fourth lines. Each stressed syllable indicates a measure called a *foot*. Therefore, this stanza can be described as having four feet in the first and third lines and three feet in the second and fourth lines.

A closer look at the feet shows that most of them consist of a single unstressed syllable followed by the stressed syllable. This combination (∪ /) is called an *iambic foot*. Although there are a few feet in every stanza that have variations, we can describe this poem as being written in an iambic rhythm.

Does "The Sprinters" show a fairly consistent rhythm like this? Analyze the first few lines to find out.

```
      ∪  /  ∪  /   ∪
1  The gun explodes them.
        /  ∪∪  / ∪∪  ∪  /
2  Pummeling, pistoning they fly
      ∪   ∪    /
3  In time's face.
      ∪ / ∪∪  /∪
4  A go at the limit,
      ∪ /∪∪ /
5  A terrible try
      ∪   /  ∪  / ∪   /
6  To smash the ticking glass
```

This poem shows much more irregularity than the first two you looked at. There is no consistent pattern of stressed and unstressed syllables. One line begins with a stressed syllable, the others with unstressed syllables. Four lines end with stressed syllables; the others end with unstressed ones. The number of unstressed syllables separating stressed ones ranges from one to three. Until line 6, there is no line that uses iambic feet throughout.

Why did the poet use such a difficult rhythm with so little flow? You can discover the reason when you read the poem aloud and listen for both the rhythm and the meaning of the words. These lines of the poem describe the beginning of a race. The runners are starting from a still position, trying to get into a strong and speedy rhythm. They are struggling, and the poet wants us to feel their struggle by pushing us from one pattern to another. A few minutes into the race, and six lines into the poem, the runners hit their stride. Notice what happens to the rhythm at that point:

$$\cup \; / \; \cup \; /$$
Outpace the beat
$$\cup \; \; / \; \; \cup \; \; / \; \cup /$$
That runs, that streaks away
$$/ \; \cup \; \; \cup \; / \cup \; \cup \; \; /$$
Tireless, and faster than they.

Now the iambic beats are clearly taking over. There are still variations, but it's easier to find a steady flow in these lines. Through the management of rhythm, the poet has given us the feeling of being in the race just by reading the poem.

EXERCISE ①

Reread the poems in Group 1. Then use what you have learned in this lesson to answer these questions:

1. Copy the second stanza of "How They Brought the Good News from Ghent to Aix," leaving space above and below each line. Then mark the stressed and unstressed syllables, following the examples in this lesson. Compare the rhythmic patterns in the second stanza with those of the first stanza above. Are they exactly the same? very similar? very different? Describe what you discover.

2. Copy the second stanza of "The Sprinters," again leaving space above and below each line. Then mark the stressed and unstressed syllables. Most of the feet are iambic, that is, composed of an unstressed syllable followed by a stressed

syllable. Identify a measure with a variation, in which the stressed syllable comes before the unstressed one. Assuming the poet had a reason for inserting that variation, what might that reason be?

Now check your answers with your teacher. Review this part of the lesson if you don't understand why an answer was incorrect.

 WRITING ON YOUR OWN ①

You have seen how poets create patterns of rhythm both to give a regular flow to a poem and to stress the meanings of passages. Now you will work with a partner to write poems with distinct rhythms. Follow these steps:

- With your partner, select a pair of animals that have very different styles of moving. For example, one good pair might be a sloth and a squirrel; another might be a giant turtle and a monkey. Briefly discuss the differences in the two animals' appearances and ways of moving. Take whatever notes that you feel will help you write your poems.
- Recall cheers that you have heard at sporting events or rallies, such as "Two, four, six, eight/Who do we appreciate?" Then choose one of the animals and write a cheer of about eight lines for it. Your partner should write a cheer about the other animal. The rhythm of your cheer must suggest the way your animal moves and must be clearly different from the rhythm of your partner's cheer. For example, if you were writing a turtle's cheer, the rhythm would plod slowly, with many stressed syllables. If you were writing a monkey's cheer, however, the rhythm would move quickly and easily, with many unstressed syllables. Your cheers need not make sense. Use invented words if you like, as long as it's obvious how to pronounce them.

- Read your cheers to each other to make sure you have used different rhythms. Revise the cheers as needed. Then, without identifying which cheer is intended for which animal, read your cheers to a classmate. Ask the classmate to match the cheer with the animal. Afterward, discuss the results and possible improvements you might make.

LESSON ② RHYME

Rhymes are words whose ending sounds are the same or very similar. Rhyming words may be spelled the same, as in *oat* and *boat*, or they may be spelled differently, as in *oat* and *wrote*. In some rhymes, either the vowel sounds or the consonant sounds are not perfect matches. For example, *full* and *gull* have slightly different vowel sounds.

Words of two or more syllables are said to rhyme if their stressed syllables and any following syllables rhyme. For example, in *perhaps* and *collapse*, the second syllable of each word is the stressed syllable, so the first syllable need not match for the words to be rhymes. However, in *neighbor*, *labor*, and *favor*, the stressed syllable in each word is the first syllable. Therefore, both syllables must end in the same or similar sounds for the words to rhyme.

Rhymes of the first type, with only one syllable or one stressed syllable, are called *masculine rhymes*. Rhymes of the second type, with a stressed syllable and one or more unstressed syllables, are called *feminine rhymes*. Feminine rhymes may consist of two or more words together, as in *highway* and *my way*.

"A Time to Talk" provides examples of both types of rhymes. *Road/hoed*, *walk/talk*, and *around/ground* are all masculine rhymes, while is *it/visit* is a feminine rhyme.

Rhymes in poems can be described according to where the rhyming words occur. A rhyme between words at the ends of two lines is called an *end rhyme*. A rhyme between two words

or phrases in the same line is called an *internal rhyme*. All of
the poems in Group 2 use end rhyme. For an example of internal rhyme, look at the third line of any stanza in "The Yarn of
the *Nancy Bell*." Here are two examples, from stanzas 2 and 4:

| And I heard this wight on the shore recite |

| For I couldn't help thinking the man had been drinking, |

Notice that the first example is a masculine rhyme, and
the second is a feminine rhyme.

Not all poems use rhyme, but in those that do, the rhyming
words are carefully placed in patterns. We track these patterns
by assigning a different letter to each rhyming ending and
recording that letter each time the ending appears. Look, for
example, at the first four lines of "Jenny Kissed Me." The letter *a* is assigned to the rhyming words *met* and *get*, and *b* is
assigned to the rhyming words *sat in* and *that in*.

Jenny kissed me when we met,	*a*
Jumping from the chair she sat in.	*b*
Time, you thief, who love to get	*a*
Sweets into your list, put that in.	*b*

Compare the *rhyme scheme*—the pattern of rhyme—in
"Jenny Kissed Me" with the pattern in "The Kiss" below. How
are the rhyme schemes similar? How are they different?

I hoped that he would love me,	*a*
And he has kissed my mouth,	*b*
But I am like a stricken bird	*c*
That cannot reach the south.	*b*

In each poem, the second and fourth lines rhyme. But in
"Jenny Kissed Me" so do the first and third lines. Only two

letters are needed to identify the rhyme scheme of this poem: *abab*. In "The Kiss," however, the first and third lines have different endings. Three letters are needed to identify the rhyme scheme: *abcb*.

For more information about the most popular combinations of patterns of rhyme and rhythm, see Unit 6.

EXERCISE ②

Reread the poems in Group 2. Then use what you have learned in this lesson to answer these questions:

1. As discussed earlier, "A Time to Talk" contains the feminine rhyme *is it/visit*. Which other poem in Group 2 uses feminine rhyme? Identify two instances of feminine rhyme in that poem.

2. Which is the most accurate description of the rhyme scheme in "A Time to Talk"—*abcdefghhe, abcadbceed,* or *abcadefggd*? Of the four poems in Group 2, "A Time to Talk" sounds the most like normal conversation. How does the rhyme scheme contribute to this effect?

3. What rhyme scheme do you find in "Song"?

Now check your answers with your teacher. Review this part of the lesson if you don't understand why an answer was incorrect.

WRITING ON YOUR OWN ②

In "Jenny Kissed Me" and "The Kiss" you saw how poets writing on the same topic used different rhythms and rhyme schemes to present different moods and conclusions. Now you and your writing partner will write separately on the same topic and compare your results. Follow these steps:

- First, choose a story that is familiar to both of you. It could be a story from a fairy tale or a movie, or it could be an event in the news.
- As a warm-up exercise, make lists of rhymes together. Take turns saying words that have some connection with the story you have chosen to write about. For example, suppose you chose *The Wizard of Oz.* You or your partner might suggest the words *lion* and *girl.* Then the two of you might come up with rhymes for lion such as *fry in, fryin', cryin', cry in, Brian,* and *tryin'.* For *girl,* you might come up with *furl, whirl, pearl,* and *curl.* Make sure your words include both masculine and feminine rhymes.
- With your partner, review "Jenny Kissed Me" and "The Kiss." Compare their rhyme schemes and their rhythms. Choose one of those rhyme schemes that both of you will match. Try to match that poem's rhythm as well. Read the poem several times to get the pattern in your head.
- Now separately, write a four-line poem on the topic that you and your partner chose. Use the rhymes from your lists as well as others. When you are both finished, exchange poems. Take turns reading the poems aloud. Let your partner know whether he or she was successful in matching the rhyme scheme and rhythm that you both chose.

LESSON ③ REPETITION

For hundreds of years, rhyme has been an important element of poetry written in English. However, it is not the only kind of repetition that can give form and pattern to poetry. In fact, when the English language was beginning to take shape, its poetry didn't use rhyme at all. Instead, it used alliteration. As you learned in Unit 1, *alliteration* is the repetition of sounds at the beginning of words, as in "Peter Piper picked a peck of pickled peppers." One of the oldest poems in the language that became English is *Beowulf*. It tells the tale of a hero who battles monsters. Instead of using a rhyme scheme, this poem follows a complex pattern of alliteration. For example, in each line the beginning sound of the third accented syllable matches that of the first or the second accented syllable, or both.

Today there are no rules governing the use of alliteration, except that the repeated sounds should appear close to each other. As a matter of fact, the repeated sounds can even appear within the same words as well as at their beginnings, as in "pickled peppers."

Why would a poet choose to use alliteration? Alliteration can call attention to a phrase, as the /f/ sounds do in this example

Full fathom five thy father lies;

Alliteration can link words within a line, or from one line to the next, as in this example:

Nothing of him that doth fade
But doth suffer a sea-change
Into something rich and strange.

It also can add emphasis to the meaning of a phrase, as in this line from "Nothing Gold Can Stay":

So dawn goes down to day.

Another kind of repetition is assonance. As you learned in Unit 1, *assonance* is the repetition of vowel sounds in words that are close together. This line from "Fireworks" contains six repetitions of the /u/ sound:

Not guns, not thunder, but a flutter of clouded drums

Like alliteration, assonance links words and gives a musical sound to lines.

Yet another kind of repetition is the repetition of whole words, phrases, or lines. Note how the repetition of the word *say* four times in "Jenny Kissed Me" builds up anticipation. The four phrases beginning with *say* prepare the reader for the delightful contrast in the final line:

> Say I'm weary, say I'm sad;
> > Say that health and wealth have missed me;
> Say I'm growing old, but add—
> > Jenny kissed me!

Many long poems use *refrains*, lines that are repeated regularly throughout the poem. For example, "The Yarn of the *Nancy Bell*" uses this entire stanza four times, with slight variations:

> "Oh, I am a cook and a captain bold,
> > And the mate of the *Nancy* brig,
> And a bo'sun tight, and a midshipmite,
> > And the crew of the captain's gig."

Just as repeated sounds in words give unity to lines and stanzas, refrains give unity to poems with many stanzas.

Poets also use *onomatopoeia* to add sound to their work. *Onomatopoeia* refers to words that imitate the sound of something. The phrases *ding-dong* and *ding-dong, bell* in "Full Fathom Five" are onomatopoetic: they suggest the sound of a bell ringing.

EXERCISE ③

Reread the poems in Group 3. Then use what you have learned in this lesson to answer these questions:

1. Identify at least three lines in "Fireworks" that use alliteration with the /s/ or /z/ sound. Write those lines and underline each letter or combination of letters that represents either sound. Why did the poet make such extensive use of those two sounds?

2. Examine line 4 of "Fireworks" for assonance. Identify all the words in this line that have the same vowel sound. Say the line aloud and listen to the words because the same sound is spelled several different ways and will not necessarily be obvious by just reading silently.

Now check your answers with your teacher. Review this part of the lesson if you don't understand why an answer was incorrect.

 WRITING ON YOUR OWN ③

In this exercise you and your partner will help each other use alliteration and assonance to link words or give them emphasis. Follow these steps:

• You have seen how poems on different topics tend to emphasize different sounds in alliteration. With your partner, select four or five consonant sounds that you feel would go well with each of these topics: bees, a garbage disposal, a race car, a violin.

• Assign one of the four topics to your partner and have him or her assign a different topic to you. On your own, write a short poem about your topic, using as much alliteration with the chosen letters as possible. Your poem may rhyme, or it can be in free verse. Try to include sensory details and figurative language. Also include at least one phrase that uses assonance.

• Exchange your completed poem with your partner. Read and comment on each other's work. Explain what you especially like about each other's poems and make any suggestions necessary for how to improve them.

DISCUSSION GUIDES

1. Discuss these questions with a small group and report the group's opinions to the class: Did you find "The Yarn of the *Nancy Bell*" disgusting or funny? How did the poet try to keep this poem about cannibalism unreal and silly? Do you think he succeeded? In general, do you believe that there are any topics that poets should not write about? Why or why not?

2. If you were including the poems in this unit in an anthology, how would you arrange them? Alone or with a partner, select only six of the 10 and sort them into three categories. Write a table of contents listing the titles of your categories and indicating the order in which you would present the poems. Later, the whole class should compare and discuss the different tables of contents that result from this activity. Are some proposed tables of contents more likely than others to get people enthusiastic about the poems? Why or why not?

3. If you were invited to read several poems from this unit to patients in a hospital, which ones would you select? Choose one of the poems and prepare it for an oral presentation, either alone or with one or two classmates. If you'd like, divide the lines in a way that contributes to the drama of the presentation. Practice reading the poem with expression. If it is short, try to memorize it. Then try out your performance on your class or part of your class. If possible, make arrangements for yourself and several performers to present your readings in a nearby hospital.

CREATE A COLLECTION OF POEMS

In this exercise you and your writing partner will create a collection of poems. The poems in your collection will contain some of the techniques that you learned about in this unit.

Follow these steps to write your poems. If you have questions about the writing process, refer to Using the Writing Process on page 232.

- Assemble the work that you and your partner did for all the writing exercises in this unit: 1) lists of words and phrases describing two or more theme-related topics, 2) two cheers whose rhythms suggest the animals they represent, 3) two original poems that use either the *abab* or *abcb* rhyme scheme, 4) a short poem that uses alliteration to suggest its topic.
- Review your lists of possible themes and topics and then agree upon one of those themes. Divide the theme's four topics so that you and your partner each have two. Before you and your partner begin writing your poems, discuss various sound effects that you both might use. You'll want your poetry collection to show a variety of techniques, so make sure you both plan to use a different technique (or techniques) in each poem.
- Write your poems. Keep them between two and ten lines each. Depending on your working style, you may want to confer with your partner while you write, or you may want to work independently. If you work independently, set up a time to discuss your poems.
- When all four poems are written, review each other's work and make any revisions that you agree will improve them.
- With your partner, arrange the four poems in the order that you feel works best. Then add any or all of the poems that you wrote for the rest of this unit. Next, write a table of contents that lists the order of all the poems in your collection.
- Using a computer, a typewriter, or your best handwriting, work with your partner to create your collection of poems. Include a title page. Make your finished collection available to your classmates.

Figurative Language

145

INTRODUCTION

ABOUT THE LESSONS

You know that poetry expresses personal thoughts and experiences by using striking language that helps others understand and appreciate them. One of the important characteristics of poetic language is that it makes unexpected connections and forces readers to see familiar situations from unfamiliar viewpoints. Poets use numerous techniques to help them make connections. In this unit you will learn about a few of those techniques—called *figurative language*, or figures of speech. You also will examine how figurative language helps make the meaning of poetry clearer.

WRITING: USING FIGURATIVE LANGUAGE

At the end of this unit you will write an original poem that uses several types of figurative language. Begin by following these steps:

- Copy the following chart onto a sheet of paper:

	Animal	Food	Toy	Item of Clothing
1. (Your Name)				
2. (Friend's Name)				
3. (Everyday Object)				
4. (Object in Nature)				

- Begin filling in the chart by replacing the words in parentheses in the first column with actual names of people and objects.
- Complete the first row of the chart by asking yourself these questions: If I were an animal, which one would I be? If I were a food, what would I be? If I were a toy, which one would I be? If I were an item of clothing, what would I be?

- Complete the chart by continuing to ask yourself the same questions about the rest of the items in the first column.
- Save your completed chart. It will help you think of figures of speech as you work through the writing exercises in this unit.

ABOUT THIS POET

Lucille Clifton (1936–   ) was born in DePew, New York. She is the great-great-granddaughter of an African woman who was brought to the United States as a slave in 1830. Clifton attended Howard University and the State University of New York College at Fredonia. As the mother of six children, she writes with understanding about the difficulties and joys of maintaining loving family relationships. In 1969 she published her first collection of poems, *Good Times: Poems*, which was named as one of the year's 10 best books by the *New York Times*.

To date, Clifton has published 11 volumes of poetry for adults and 19 books for children. In seven of her 19 children's books she tells the story of Everett Anderson, a fictional African-American boy living in an urban neighborhood. Much of Clifton's writing reflects her pride in her cultural heritage, her concern for African-American youth in America, her satisfaction in being a woman, and the importance of family ties.

AS YOU READ

As you read each poem in this unit, ask yourself the following questions:

- What unusual comparison (if any) does this poem contain? What do the two items in the comparison have in common?
- Why might the poet have chosen to make this particular comparison? How does the comparison help express the poet's ideas and feelings?

Identity

by Julio Noboa Polanco

ABOUT THE SELECTION

Julio Noboa Polanco (1949–   ) is a bilingual poet of Puerto Rican heritage. Born in the Bronx, he has earned degrees in anthropology and education. He now lives in Texas, where he is a writer for a national policy institute on Latino affairs. Before Polanco graduated from high school, his family moved to Chicago. He was still in school there when he wrote "Identity."

Let them be as flowers,
always watered, fed, guarded, admired,
but harnessed[1] to a pot of dirt.

I'd rather be a tall, ugly weed,
clinging on cliffs, like an eagle
wind-wavering above high, jagged rocks.

To have broken through the surface of stone,
to live, to feel exposed to the madness
of the vast, eternal sky.
To be swayed by the breezes of an ancient sea,
carrying my soul, my seed, beyond the mountains of time
or into the abyss[2] of the bizarre.[3]
I'd rather be unseen, and if

---

[1] fastened, as a horse to a plow

[2] an immeasurable depth

[3] things strikingly unconventional and strange

then shunned by everyone,
than to be a pleasant-smelling flower,
growing in clusters in the fertile valley,
where they're praised, handled, and plucked
by greedy, human hands.

I'd rather smell of musty, green stench
than of sweet, fragrant lilac.
If I could stand alone, strong and free,
I'd rather be a tall, ugly weed.

Mama Is a Sunrise

by Evelyn Tooley Hunt

ABOUT THE SELECTION

As you read Evelyn Tooley Hunt's poem "Mama Is a Sunrise," look for clues that identify the setting. Think about how the same ideas would be worded in your part of the country.

When she comes slip-footing through the door,
    she kindles us
    like lump coal lighted,
    and we wake up glowing.
She puts a spark even in Papa's eyes
and turns out all our darkness.

When she comes sweet-talking in the room,
    she warms us
    like grits[1] and gravy,
    and we rise up shining.
Even at night-time Mama is a sunrise
that promises tomorrow and tomorrow.

---

[1] corn meal that is boiled and served as a breakfast food or side dish

First Snow

by Ted Kooser

ABOUT THE SELECTION

Ted Kooser (1939–   ) combines his poetry writing with a career in marketing life insurance. Born in Ames, Iowa, he earned degrees from Iowa State University and the University of Nebraska. He has published nine collections of his own poems and has had poems included in two other collections. He also has edited a poetry anthology. His work has been honored with two fellowships from the National Endowment for the Arts. Like most of Kooser's poems, "First Snow" is set on the Great Plains of North America.

The old black dog comes in one evening
with the first few snowflakes on his back
and falls asleep, throwing his bad leg out
at our excitement. This is the night
when one of us gets to say, as if it were news,
that no two snowflakes are ever alike;
the night when each of us remembers something
snowier. The kitchen is a kindergarten
steamy with stories. The dog gets stiffly up
and limps away, seeking a quiet spot
at the heart of the house. Outside,
in silence, with diamonds in his fur,
the winter night curls round the legs of the trees,
sleepily blinking snowflakes from his lashes.

Check

by James Stephens

ABOUT THE SELECTION

Among the many meanings of the word *check* are these: an abrupt stop in forward movement; the condition of being stopped or held back; in sports, the act of blocking an opponent. Which of these meanings, if any, do you suppose James Stephens (1882–1950) had in mind when he named this poem?

The Night was creeping on the ground!
She crept, and did not make a sound

Until she reached the tree: And then
She covered it, and stole again

Along the grass beside the wall!
—I heard the rustling of her shawl

As she threw blackness everywhere
Along the sky, the ground, the air,

And in the room where I was hid!
But, no matter what she did

To everything that was without,
She could not put my candle out!

So I stared at the Night! And she
Stared back solemnly at me!

Hockey

by Scott Blaine

ABOUT THE SELECTION

Anyone who's ever played or watched a no-holds-barred game of hockey knows how exciting it can be. As players send the puck flying all over the ice, the whole game can change in an instant. Scott Blaine's "Hockey" uses strong comparisons to capture the rush of such a moment.

The ice is smooth, smooth, smooth.
The air bites to the center
Of warmth and flesh, and I whirl.
It begins in a game . . .
The puck swims, skims, veers,
Goes leading my vision
Beyond the chasing reach of my stick.

The air is sharp, steel-sharp.
I suck needles of breathing,
And feel the players converge.[1]
It grows to a science . . .
We clot, break, drive,
Electrons in motion
In the magnetic pull of the puck.

The play is fast, fierce, tense.
Sticks click and snap like teeth
Of wolves on the scent of a prey.
It ends in the kill . . .
I am one of the pack in a mad,
Taut[2] leap of desperation
In the wild, slashing drive for the goal.

---

[1] come together from different directions

[2] tight

Hide and Seek

by Sara Teasdale

ABOUT THE SELECTION

Sara Teasdale (1884–1933) was one of the most popular poets of the early twentieth century. She was born in St. Louis, Missouri, and educated at home. Then she traveled widely in Europe and the Near East before settling in New York City and devoting herself to writing poetry. Frequently ill, she preferred to live apart from society. Her poems were so popular that one collection, *Love Songs* (published in 1917), went through five editions in one year. Because of this, she was awarded the first Pulitzer Prize for poetry in 1918. Teasdale felt that poetry should reach out to the reader in such a way that "the reader will feel and not think while he is reading." What emotion do you feel as you read "Hide and Seek"?

When I was a child we played sometimes in the dark;
    Hide and seek in the dark is a terrible game,
With the nerves pulled tight in fear of the stealthy[1] seeker,
    With the brief exultance,[2] and the blood in the veins
  like flame.

Now I see that life is a game in the dark,
    A groping in shadows, a brief exultance, a dread
Of what may crouch beside us or lurk behind us,
    A leaving of what we want to say unsaid,
Sure of one thing only, a long sleep
When the game is over and we are put to bed.

---

[1] cautious and secret to avoid being noticed

[2] joy; triumph

the mississippi river empties into the gulf

by Lucille Clifton

ABOUT THE SELECTION

Lucille Clifton (1936–   ) was born in DePew, New York. Much of her writing has been influenced by her being an African American and a mother of six children. Since 1969 she has published 11 volumes of poetry for adults and 19 books for children. For more information about Clifton, see About This Poet at the beginning of this unit.

   The lack of capitalization in "the mississippi river flows into the gulf" is characteristic of many of Clifton's poems. Note that the title of this poem is also, in effect, its first line. Without it, the poem could be rather confusing.

and the gulf enters the sea and so forth,
none of them emptying anything,
all of them carrying yesterday
forever on their white tipped backs,
all of them dragging forward tomorrow.
it is the great circulation[1]
of the earth's body, like the blood
of the gods, this river in which the past
is always flowing. every water
is the same water coming round.
everyday someone is standing on the edge
of this river, staring into time,
whispering mistakenly:
only here. only now.

---

[1] movement in a circle or circuit, especially the movement of blood through the body's vessels due to the pumping action of the heart

UNDERSTANDING THE POEMS

Record your answers to these questions in your personal literature notebook. Follow the directions for each group.

GROUP 1   Reread the poems in Group 1 to complete these sentences.

Reviewing the Selection

1. On the surface, the speaker of "Identity" has a poor opinion of
  a. tall, ugly weeds.
  b. eagles.
  c. the breezes of an ancient sea.
  d. flowers.

Interpreting the Selection

2. The time of day described in "Check" is
  a. nightfall.
  b. midnight.
  c. daybreak.
  d. noon.

3. When the speaker in "First Snow" says that the "kitchen is a kindergarten," he or she means that
  a. the room is full of five-year-olds.
  b. the speaker's parents are teaching him or her in the kitchen.
  c. in his or her memory, the speaker is confusing the kitchen with kindergarten.
  d. the adults are as excited as five-year-olds telling stories.

Recognizing How Words Are Used

4. In "Mama Is a Sunrise" the word that suggests graceful movement is
  a. *promises.*
  b. *slip-footing.*
  c. *kindles.*
  d. *shining.*

Appreciating Poetry

5. All four poems in Group 1 appeal to the sense of sight. In addition, one poem appeals to the sense of smell. Which poem does so?

a. "Check"

b. "Identity"

c. "First Snow"

d. "Mama Is a Sunrise"

GROUP 2 Reread the poems in Group 2 to complete these sentences.

Reviewing the Selection

6. The speaker in "Hockey" is most probably

a. an amateur hockey player.

b. a professional hockey player.

c. a spectator at a hockey game.

d. a scientist analyzing a hockey game.

Interpreting the Selection

7. In the lines "all of them carrying yesterday/forever on their white tipped backs" from the poem "the mississippi river empties into the gulf," the pronouns *them* and *their* refer to

a. large fish in the waters of the gulf.

b. various bodies of water.

c. boats on the gulf.

d. swimmers in the waters of the gulf.

8. "Hide and Seek" compares death to

a. the game of hide and seek.

b. the darkness in which the speaker used to play the game.

c. going to bed after the game.

d. the "seeker" who tries to find the speaker in the dark.

Recognizing How Words Are Used

9. In "Hockey" there is an example of rhyme in the line

a. The ice is smooth, smooth, smooth.

b. The puck swims, skims, veers.

c. In the magnetic pull of the puck.

d. We clot, break, drive.

Appreciating Poetry

10. The poem "the mississippi river empties into the gulf"

    a. uses traditional verse form, with rhyme and a clear rhythm.

    b. uses conventional capitalization and punctuation.

    c. expresses an idea from a unique point of view.

    d. does none of the above.

Now check your answers with your teacher. Study the questions you answered incorrectly. What types of questions were they? Talk with your teacher about ways to work on those skills.

Figurative Language

You've probably heard this advertising slogan: "A day without orange juice is like a day without sunshine." It leaves the listener with a pleasant, warm feeling about orange juice. After all, the thinking goes, everyone enjoys a day with sunshine, so everyone must enjoy a day with orange juice too. This slogan is an example of a type of figurative language—language that compares two things that are like each other in some way. The comparison in this slogan is between orange juice and sunshine. These two things are being compared because both orange juice and the sun provide us with needed vitamins. The comparison does not state this scientific fact, however. Instead, it leads listeners to think of all the pleasures associated with a sunny day. The advertisers hope that listeners will make the connection, then, between orange juice and pleasure. The orange growers and their ad agency could have said, "An orange is like the sun" or "An orange is the sun." However, these comparisons would not have made listeners equate orange juice with the idea of pleasure.

There are many ways in which poets use figurative language to help readers make connections. This unit will discuss the following uses of figurative language:

- Poets use figurative language, or figures of speech, to help readers look at common objects or ideas in uncommon ways.
- Poets use figurative language to help readers better understand and appreciate their poems.

LESSON 1   FIGURES OF SPEECH

Figures of speech are words or phrases that create strong images in readers' minds. Some figures of speech compare unlike things or ideas. A *simile* compares two things using the word *like* or *as*. "Identity," for example, begins with this simile:

159

Let them be as flowers,
always watered, fed, guarded, admired,
but harnessed to a pot of dirt.

In this simile, the poet is comparing some people to flowers. He claims they are alike in that they are both cared for and admired, but they are also both tied down—the flowers by the soil and a pot and people by life and responsibilities.

A *metaphor* compares two things without using *like* or *as*. Instead, it may say that one thing is the other. "Mama Is a Sunrise" uses a metaphor in its title and then goes on to explain the similarities between "Mama" and a sunrise:

She puts a spark even in Papa's eyes
and turns out all our darkness.

Even at night-time Mama is a sunrise
that promises tomorrow and tomorrow.

Just like a sunrise, Mama turns out the darkness and always brings the promise of a new day.

Some metaphors make comparisons without even using the verb *to be*. Note, for example, how "First Snow" describes a winter night:

. . . Outside,
in silence, with diamonds in his fur,
the winter night curls round the legs of the trees,
sleepily blinking snowflakes from his lashes.

The poem never says that the winter night *is* a furry animal. However, it does say the night has fur and eyelashes, that it curls around the legs of the trees, and that it is sleepy—all of which are characteristic of an animal. The poet relies on the reader to use these clues to make the connection.

The metaphor found in "First Snow" is an example of an

implied metaphor. In an implied metaphor, only one part of the comparison is stated and the reader must use context to figure out the other part of the comparison.

Sometimes an entire poem or an extended passage of a poem develops a single metaphor in depth. When this happens, it is called an *extended metaphor.* "Identity" is an example of an extended metaphor. Throughout the poem the speaker compares him- or herself to a weed and then describes a weed's existence:

> To have broken through the surface of stone,
> to live, to feel exposed to the madness
> of the vast, eternal sky.
> To be swayed by the breezes of an ancient sea,
> carrying my soul, my seed, beyond the mountains of time
> or into the abyss of the bizarre.

Personification is another kind of figure of speech, which gives human characteristics to animals, things, or ideas. In the following example from "Check," the poet personifies night as a mysterious, dark woman:

> I heard the rustling of her shawl
>
> As she threw blackness everywhere
> Along the sky, the ground, the air,
>
> And in the room where I was hid!

The poet paints a haunting picture of the nonhuman night as a woman in a shawl who "threw blackness everywhere."

EXERCISE ①
Reread the poems in Group 1. Then use what you have learned in this lesson to answer these questions:

1. Identify two similes in "Mama Is a Sunrise." Explain how the two items in each comparison are alike.

2. Review "Check." Explain how the lines of the poem use metaphor to describe the gradual stages of night falling.

> And the wide road curving on to China or
>   Kansas City or perhaps Calcutta,
> Had withered to a crooked path of dust

Now check your answers with your teacher. Review this part of the lesson if you don't understand why an answer was incorrect.

WRITING ON YOUR OWN (1)

In this lesson you learned about several figures of speech. Now you will write a few of your own. Follow these steps:

- Reread the chart that you created in the first writing exercise. Choose one of the comparisons on the chart and use it to write a simile. For example, if you compared yourself to a tuxedo, you could write "I am like a tuxedo. I am always full of class and style."
- Choose another comparison from the chart and use it to write a metaphor. For example, if you compared clouds to mashed potatoes, you could write "My mashed potatoes were soft clouds floating across a sky-blue plate."
- Choose two more comparisons from the chart and use them to write one example of personification and one extended metaphor.
- Save all your figures of speech. You may use them in a poem you will write at the end of this unit.

LESSON ② THE IMPACT OF FIGURATIVE LANGUAGE

Using figurative language effectively can take a bit of work. After all, even using normal, everyday language can be difficult. A problem both types of language face is that we connect feelings as well as literal meanings to words.

Every word has a specific meaning that is defined in the dictionary. This meaning is called its *denotation*. In addition, the word may suggest a feeling, either positive or negative. This additional meaning is called the word's *connotation*. For example, the words *slender* and *skinny* have similar dictionary meanings, but most people would rather be called *slender* than *skinny*. *Slender* has a positive connotation, while *skinny* has a more negative one. If you were to comment on a friend's appearance by saying, "You look so skinny," your friend would probably feel insulted. On the other hand, if you were to say "You look so slender," your friend would probably take it as a compliment.

Similarly, a poet must be selective in creating just the right figure of speech. A metaphor, for example, must be unexpected and surprising in order to gain the reader's full attention. But it also must have a logic to it. The two items being compared must have something in common that the typical reader can recognize or the metaphor will be confusing and useless. Furthermore, the connotations of the figure of speech must support the idea or feeling the poet is trying to express.

Take a look at "Hockey" to see how effectively and appropriately figures of speech contribute to its meaning, mood, and success. The first stanza begins with a realistic description of an ice rink. The speaker notes the smooth ice, the biting air, and his or her own movement on the ice. But with the beginning of the game comes the first metaphor:

It begins in a game . . .
The puck swims, skims, veers,
Goes leading my vision
Beyond the chasing reach of my stick.

The puck is described as if it were a living creature acting on its own. The speaker doesn't mention other human players. Instead, the game seems to be between the speaker and the puck.

In the second stanza, the air is no longer merely biting. It is "steel-sharp," and the speaker sucks in "needles of breathing." The words *steel* and *needles* suggest technology or science rather than a game, leading naturally into the next metaphor:

> It grows to a science . . .
> We clot, break, drive,
> Electrons in motion
> In the magnetic pull of the puck.

Now that the game has become a science, the players are no longer acting on their own. They are under the control of the puck, which is described as a force with a "magnetic pull." The speaker has lost his or her identity as a human and has become a mere electron.

The third stanza begins with the words "The play," but what follows doesn't suggest play. Notice how so many words in the stanza have connotations of out-of-control violence, stressing the new metaphor of players as frenzied animals: *fierce, click and snap, teeth, scent, prey, the kill, the pack, mad, desperation, wild, slashing*. The players, who lost control of their actions in the second stanza, are no longer playing a game:

> It ends in the kill . . .
> I am one of the pack in a mad,
> Taut leap of desperation
> In the wild, slashing drive for the goal.

In "Hockey," the figurative language does not merely make the poet's message more interesting. The progression from one metaphor to another helps to express the message more clearly and precisely. It also helps readers experience the tension that the speaker feels during the game.

Although not every poem relies so heavily on its figures of

speech, whatever figurative language you see in a poem is there for a purpose. Your enjoyment of any poem will be enriched by a careful look at the part its figures of speech play.

EXERCISE ②

Reread the poems in Group 2. Then use what you have learned in this lesson to answer these questions:

1. To what is life compared in the poem "Hide and Seek"? To what is death compared? What attitude toward death is suggested by the connotations of these figures of speech?

2. What is the central metaphor of "the mississippi river empties into the gulf"? What connotations are suggested by the additional simile "like the blood of the gods"? With these figures of speech in mind, reread the last four lines. What do you think the theme of this poem is?

WRITING ON YOUR OWN ②

In this exercise you will use figurative language to express positive and negative connotations. Follow these steps:

- Go back to your chart and choose one of the comparisons on it. For example, you might choose the comparison between your friend and a cat. Then write a figure of speech that compares your friend to a cat in a positive way. For example, you might write "Ashley was a cat gliding gracefully down the hall." The words *gliding gracefully* give this metaphor a positive connotation. They suggest that Ashley moves with ease and beauty.
- Now write a figure of speech that compares your friend to a cat in a negative way. For example, you might write "Ashley is like a cat, always proud and aloof." The words *proud* and *aloof* give this simile a negative connotation. They suggest that Ashley is somewhat conceited and keeps a distance between herself and others.
- Save your figures of speech for the last writing exercise.

DISCUSSION GUIDES

1. Do you believe that "Hockey" presents an accurate view of what can happen in a fast-paced game? Do the players sometimes act like animals in their desire to win, or has the poet exaggerated the situation for a dramatic effect? Discuss these questions with your class. What do most students think?

2. The poems in this unit vary widely in mood. With a small group, categorize the poems according to mood. Try to create no more than five categories. If a poem doesn't fit with any of the others, find a poem somewhere else in this book that could be matched with it. Then compare your group's categories with those of other groups. Did any of the groups come up with similar categories? Did they assign the individual poems in similar ways? What do you suppose explains the differences?

3. You probably have noticed from the biographical notes that many poets have interests and abilities in other fields of fine art, such as dance, photography, and music. You can link poetry and another field of art too. Select a favorite poem from this unit and express its theme or mood in another medium. For example, suppose you choose to express a poem through music. You might pair it with a popular song, a classical piece, an original tune, or a medley of different passages that you could play while you read the poem aloud. To express a certain poem through art, you might draw, paint, or sculpt a piece that reflects the poem's message and mood. Work independently or with a group of classmates to prepare your presentation. Then, if possible, display your work in a multimedia presentation or a gallery display.

WRITE A POEM CONTAINING FIGURES OF SPEECH

In this unit you have examined different figures of speech and how they are used in poetry. Now you will use what you have learned to write an original poem that uses two or more figures of speech.

Follow these steps to write your poem. If you have questions about the writing process, refer to Using the Writing Process on page 232.

- Assemble and review the work you did for all the writing exercises in this unit: 1) a chart that compares different people and things; 2) four original figures of speech—a simile, a metaphor, an example of personification, and an extended metaphor; 3) two comparisons—one with a positive connotation and one with a negative connotation.

- Review your chart and all of your writing assignments. Then decide which comparison or comparisons would make the best subject for a poem.

- Write a free-verse or rhyming poem describing your chosen subject. Use any of the figures of speech that you wrote earlier in the unit or make up new ones to describe your subject. If possible, include alliteration, assonance, or both to add interest to your words. Try to keep your poem to twelve lines or fewer.

- Ask a classmate to read your poem and identify its figures of speech. If you have used a simile, a metaphor, or personification, can your classmate identify the two things being compared? Can he or she identify words that give your comparisons positive or negative connotations? Revise your poem as needed, based on your classmate's comments.

- Proofread your poem for grammar and spelling errors. Then make a final copy and save it in your writing portfolio.

Form in Poetry

INTRODUCTION

ABOUT THE LESSONS

In Unit 1 you briefly examined the distinctive appearance of poetry. In Unit 4 you looked at how rhythm, rhyme, and repetition give a sense of unity to a poem. In this unit you will take a closer look at patterns of rhythm and rhyme, as well as additional ways that poets give shape to their works. The poems in Group 1 show different patterns of rhythm and rhyme, while the poems in Group 2 illustrate some different forms of poetry.

 WRITING: USING FORM IN POETRY

Rhythms are important outside of poetry as well. The following activity will help you become aware of rhythmic patterns and their effects on speech and other forms of writing.

- Certain lines from speeches and nonfiction writing attain lasting fame on their own. For example, memorable lines from historical figures include Julius Caesar's "I came, I saw, I conquered"; Abraham Lincoln's "Four score and seven years ago"; and Neil Armstrong's "The *Eagle* has landed." One thing that makes these lines easy to say and remember is their rhythm—that is, their repeated pattern of stressed and unstressed syllables. Start a list of famous lines from history. Add to the list as you read, hear, or recall a line that stands out. Mark the stressed syllables with a slanted line (/) and the unstressed syllables with a curved line (∪). Identify which of the famous lines have rhythmic patterns.
- Advertisers try to create slogans that are distinctive and easy to remember. Often, a good slogan has a clear, definite rhythm. Start a list of slogans that you hear or read in broadcast or print advertising. Mark the stressed and unstressed syllables to identify the slogans' rhythms.
- Compare your lists and findings with your classmates' lists.

ABOUT THIS POET

May Swenson (1919–1989) was born in Logan, Utah, and graduated from Utah State University. After moving to New York City she worked as an editor and then as a writer-in-residence at a number of universities in both the United States and Canada. Two of the many awards she received are the William Rose Benét Prize of the Poetry Society of America and the Bollingen Poetry Award. She also received nominations for the National Book award in 1978 and the National Book Critics Circle award in 1987.

Swenson was well-known for her complex and experimental approach to poetry. She believed that the shape of a poem contributed to its meaning, and she often wrote her poems in the shapes of the objects she was writing about. She enjoyed including puns and wordplay, and she used images and figurative language to help convey her themes. She believed that poetry is "based in a craving to get through the curtains of things as they appear, to things as they are, and then into the larger, wilder space of things as they are becoming."

In addition to writing poetry, Swenson wrote a one-act play called *The Floor*, which was first produced in 1966. Creative, inventive, and precise, Swenson was one of the most popular and successful American poets of the 20th century.

AS YOU READ

As you read the poems in this unit, ask yourself the following questions:

- What form does each poem take? Are there any poem forms, or patterns, that are more popular than others? How do I recognize and describe them?
- Are there forms of poems that have more rules than others? What sorts of rules do they follow?

An Elegy[1] on the Death of a Mad Dog

by Oliver Goldsmith

ABOUT THE SELECTION

Oliver Goldsmith (1730?–1774) was an English poet, playwright, novelist, and essayist noted for his lively style of writing. He was born in Ballymahon, Ireland, and studied medicine in Scotland before settling in England, where he supported himself by writing. His most famous works include the classic comedic play *She Stoops to Conquer* and the uplifting novel *The Vicar of Wakefield.* The humorous poem below is taken from *The Vicar of Wakefield.*

Good people all, of every sort,
    Give ear unto my song;
And if you find it wond'rous short,
    It cannot hold you long.

In Islington there was a man,
    Of whom the world might say,
That still a godly race he ran,
    Whene'er he went to pray.

A kind and gentle heart he had,
    To comfort friends and foes;
The naked every day he clad,
    When he put on his clothes.

---

[1] poem composed specifically to mourn a dead person

And in that town a dog was found,
    As many dogs there be,
Both mongrel, puppy, whelp, and hound,
    And curs of low degree.

This dog and man at first were friends;
    But when a pique[2] began,
The dog, to gain some private ends,
    Went mad and bit the man.

Around from all the neighboring streets
    The wond'ring neighbors ran,
And swore the dog had lost its wits,
    To bite so good a man.

The wound it seem'd both sore and sad
    To every Christian eye;
And while they swore the dog was mad,
    They swore the man would die.

But soon a wonder came to light,
    That showed the rogues they lied:
The man recover'd of the bite,
    The dog it was that died.

---

[2] state of irritation caused by feelings of hurt pride

The Eagle That Is Forgotten

by Vachel Lindsay

ABOUT THE SELECTION

Vachel Lindsay (1879–1931) was born in Springfield, Illinois, and studied art before becoming a poet. After a tour during which he gave readings of his poems, he developed a theatrical style of poetry intended to be performed rather than merely read. Sometimes he even included stage directions.

Many of Lindsay's poems show his love of democracy. This poem is dedicated to Illinois reformer John Altgeld, who was originally a judge in Chicago. After Altgeld was elected governor in 1893, he pardoned several workers who had been sent to prison for their part in the Haymarket Riot of 1886, a major event in the labor movement. Altgeld felt that the men had been convicted unfairly. Business owners and newspapers, however, attacked Altgeld and prevented his re-election. When he died nine years later, mostly forgotten, Lindsay honored his memory with the following poem.

(John P. Altgeld. Born December 30, 1847; died March 12, 1902)

Sleep softly . . . eagle forgotten . . . under the stone.
Time has its way with you there, and the clay has its own.

"We have buried him now," thought your foes, and in secret
    rejoiced.
They made a brave show of their mourning, their hatred
    unvoiced.
They had snarled at you, barked at you, foamed at you day
    after day.
Now you were ended. They praised you, . . . and laid you away.

The others that mourned you in silence and terror and truth,
The widow bereft[1] of her crust, and the boy without youth,
The mocked and the scorned and the wounded, the lame and
     the poor
That should have remembered forever, . . . remember no more.

Where are those lovers of yours, on what name do they call
The lost, that in armies wept over your funeral pall?
They call on the names of a hundred high-valiant ones,
A hundred white eagles have risen the sons of your sons,
The zeal in their wings is a zeal that your dreaming began
The valor that wore out your soul in the service of man.

Sleep softly, . . . eagle forgotten, . . . under the stone,
Time has its way with you there and the clay has its own.
Sleep on, O brave-hearted, O wise man, that kindled the
     flame—
To live in mankind is far more than to live in a name,
To live in mankind, far, far more . . . than to live in a name.

---

[1] having had something taken away

When, in Disgrace with Fortune and Men's Eyes

by William Shakespeare

ABOUT THE SELECTION

Although best known for his plays, William Shakespeare (1564–1616) also wrote narrative poems and over 150 sonnets—poems having 14 lines. Shakespeare was born in the town of Stratford-upon-Avon, England. After he married, he went to London to become an actor and a playwright.

Shakespeare probably produced his sonnets over a period of many years, but in 1609 they were all published together. In this collection, individual poems were not titled but were given numbers instead. The poem here is known by its first line or as Sonnet 29.

When, in disgrace with fortune and men's eyes,
I all alone beweep my outcast state,
And trouble deaf heaven with my bootless[1] cries,
And look upon myself, and curse my fate,
Wishing me like to one more rich in hope,
Featured like him, like him with friends possessed,
Desiring this man's art, and that man's scope,[2]
With what I most enjoy contented least;
Yet in these thoughts myself almost despising,
Haply I think on thee, and then my state,[3]
Like to the lark at break of day arising
From sullen earth, sings hymns at heaven's gate;
    For thy sweet love remembered such wealth brings
    That then I scorn to change my state with kings.

---

[1] useless
[2] range of a person's thoughts, abilities, or actions
[3] condition

Composed upon Westminster Bridge, September 3, 1802

by William Wordsworth

ABOUT THE SELECTION

William Wordsworth (1770–1850) was one of the most influential English poets of the last 200 years. He was born and raised in Cumberland, England, and educated at Cambridge. In 1795 he met the poet Samuel Taylor Coleridge, and together they produced a collection of poems called *Lyrical Ballads*. This book, published in 1798, is considered the beginning of the English romantic movement. Wordsworth and Coleridge abandoned the formal language used in poetry up to that time and adopted the words and rhythms of everyday speech. They saw a relationship between human thought and nature and believed that poetry should grow out of powerful feelings. All of these traits of the romantic movement are evident in the sonnet presented here.

Earth has not anything to show more fair:
Dull would he be of soul who could pass by
A sight so touching in its majesty:
This City now doth, like a garment, wear
The beauty of the morning; silent, bare,
Ships, towers, domes, theaters, and temples lie
Open unto the fields, and to the sky;
Ah bright and glittering in the smokeless air.
Never did sun more beautifully steep
In his first splendor, valley, rock, or hill;
Ne'er saw I, never felt, a calm so deep!
The river glideth at his own sweet will:
Dear God! the very houses seem asleep;
And all that mighty heart is lying still!

Two Haiku

by Matsuo Bashō, *translated by Harry Behn*

**ABOUT THE
SELECTION**

Matsuo Bashō (1644–1694) is recognized as the greatest of all writers of haiku, a kind of Japanese poetry. He was born near Kyoto, Japan, into a family that was part of the *samurai,* or warrior class. As a child he was taken into a nobleman's house to be a servant to the man's son. There he learned much and began writing haiku by the time he was nine. He continued to write for the rest of his life and wrote his best poems after 1680. The haiku on this page do not have individual titles because, according to tradition, a good haiku does not need a title.

Clouds now and then
Giving men relief
From moon-viewing.

An old silent pond . . .
A frog jumps into the pond,
    splash! Silence again.

ABOUT THE SELECTION

Much of May Swenson's work relies on wordplay and unexpected combinations. "Unconscious Came a Beauty" is one of her shaped poems, which she called *iconographs*. For more information about Swenson, see About This Poet at the beginning of this unit.

Unconscious
    came a beauty to my
  wrist
  and stopped my pencil,
    merged its shadow profile with
  my hand's ghost
  on the page:
  Red Spotted Purple or else Mourning
Cloak,[1]
paired thin-as-paper wings, near black,
were edged on the seam side poppy orange,
as were its spots.

UNCONSCIOUS

CAME A BEAUTY

I sat arrested, for its soot-haired
body's worm
shone in the sun.
It bent its tongue long as
  a leg
  black on my skin
    and clung without my
    feeling,
      while its tomb stained
        duplicate parts of
          a window opened.
          And then I
          moved.

May Swenson

Medicine

by Alice Walker

ABOUT THE SELECTION

Alice Walker (1944–   ) is best known as a novelist. However, she is also a poet, a writer of children's books and adult nonfiction, a lecturer, and an editor. Born in Eatonton, Georgia, she graduated from Sarah Lawrence College. She began winning attention and prizes with her first publications and received the Pulitzer Prize in 1983 for her novel *The Color Purple,* which was later made into a film. In much of her work, Walker focuses on the problems and triumphs of African-American women. In "Medicine," as in many of her other works, she describes a woman's devotion to her partner.

Grandma sleeps with
my sick
     grand-
pa so she
can get him
during the night
medicine
to stop
  the pain

  In
the morning
  clumsily
    I
wake
  them

Her eyes
look at me
from under-
        neath
his withered
arm

       The
     medicine
      is all
        in
     her long
       un-
           braided
              hair.

Miracles

by Walt Whitman

ABOUT THE SELECTION

Walt Whitman (1819–1892) is still considered one of America's greatest poets. Many of his poems praise the United States and its system of democracy, which he thought would improve the human race. Whitman was born on Long Island, New York, grew up in Brooklyn, and later worked as a schoolteacher, a printer, and a journalist. During the Civil War he was a government clerk and volunteered at military hospitals. He had to resign from his government work in 1873 after having a stroke, but he continued to write for many years. In his poem "Miracles," Whitman displays his typical enthusiasm for life. For more information about Whitman, see About This Poet at the beginning of Unit 1.

Why, who makes much of a miracle?
As to me I know of nothing else but miracles,
Whether I walk the streets of Manhattan,
Or dart my sight over the roofs of houses toward the sky,
Or wade with naked feet along the beach just in the edge of
     the water,
Or stand under trees in the woods,
Or talk by day with any one I love . . .
Or sit at table at dinner with the rest,
Or look at strangers opposite me riding in the car,
Or watch honeybees busy around the hive of a summer
     forenoon
Or animals feeding in the fields,
Or birds, or the wonderfulness of insects in the air,

Or the wonderfulness of the sundown, or of stars shining
     so quiet and bright,
Or the exquisite delicate thin curve of the new moon in
     spring;
These with the rest, one and all, are to me miracles,
The whole referring, yet each distinct and in its place.

To me every hour of the light and dark is a miracle,
Every cubic inch of space is a miracle,
Every square yard of the surface of the earth is spread with
     the same,
Every foot of the interior swarms with the same.

To me the sea is a continual miracle,
The fishes that swim—the rocks—the motion of the waves—
     the ships with men in them,
What stranger miracles are there?

UNDERSTANDING THE POEMS

Record your answers to these questions in your personal literature notebook. Follow the directions for each group.

GROUP 1   Reread the poems in Group 1 to complete these sentences.

Reviewing the Selection

1. The speaker in "An Elegy on the Death of a Mad Dog" blames the dog's death on the
   a. dog's bad temper.
   b. man that the dog bit.
   c. other dogs that the dog fought with.
   d. "wond'ring neighbors."

2. At the end of the poem, the speaker in "When, in Disgrace with Fortune and Men's Eyes"
   a. decides that he is happier as he is than even kings are.
   b. admits that he has even more money than a king.
   c. declares that he looks down on his king.
   d. says that the person he loves brings him gifts of money.

Interpreting the Selection

3. In "The Eagle That Is Forgotten" when the speaker says that Altgeld's foes "had snarled at you, barked at you, foamed at you," he or she means that
   a. Altgeld was killed by a pack of wild dogs.
   b. Altgeld angered people so much that they made noises like dogs.
   c. Altgeld's critics acted like vicious, unreasonable animals.
   d. eagles and dogs don't get along well.

Recognizing How Words Are Used

4. In the first line of "When, in Disgrace with Fortune and Men's Eyes" the terms *fortune* and *men's eyes* refer to
   a. a great deal of money and the organs of sight
   b. a great deal of money and reputation
   c. chance or fate and the organs of sight
   d. chance or fate and reputation

Appreciating Poetry

5. "The Eagle That Is Forgotten" is valuable to modern readers because of
   a. its historical references.
   b. its argument that a person lives on in those he or she has influenced.
   c. its tone of anger with Altgeld's accusers.
   d. the biographical information in its dedication.

GROUP 2   Reread the poems in Group 2 to complete these sentences.

Reviewing the Selection

6. "Composed upon Westminster Bridge, September 3, 1802" describes the city of London and its surroundings
   a. at dawn.
   b. at noon.
   c. at dusk.
   d. after dark.

7. The haiku beginning "An old silent pond . . ." appeals most strongly to the sense of
   a. sight.
   b. smell.
   c. hearing.
   d. touch.

Interpreting the Selection

8. The central theme of "Medicine" is that
   a. old people don't remember to take their medicine.
   b. people should take better care of their grandparents.
   c. love is the strongest medicine.
   d. doctors often prescribe the wrong medicine.

Recognizing How Words Are Used

9. In "Unconscious Came a Beauty" the phrase "my hand's ghost" refers to
   a. a ghost that had taken over just one part of the speaker's body.
   b. the drawing of a ghost that the speaker was drawing.
   c. the fact that the speaker's hand was as pale as a ghost.
   d. the shadow of the speaker's hand.

Appreciating Poetry **10.** The technique that is most noticeable in "Miracles" is the poet's

   a. repeating phrases that begin with the words *or, every,* and *to me.*

   b. repeating the beginning sounds of words.

   c. repeating the ending sounds of words.

   d. use of surprising and far-fetched comparisons.

Now check your answers with your teacher. Study the questions you answered incorrectly. What types of questions were they? Talk with your teacher about ways to work on those skills.

Form in Poetry

Since the time of Walt Whitman, many poets have rejected traditional patterns of rhyme and rhythm. These poets have felt that the old rules limit their writing and make it sound artificial. Other poets, however, appreciate the structure that traditional patterns offer. These poets enjoy the challenge of fitting ideas together in a set pattern, and they enjoy the musical quality of a traditional verse. Whether you agree with the first group of poets or the second, you will have a greater appreciation of *all* poets when you understand the forms of poetry they work with.

The lessons in this unit discuss traditional rhythmic patterns and rhyme schemes and look at both traditional and modern forms of poetry. The lessons will focus on these points:

- Poets use a variety of rhythms and rhyme schemes in their poetry.
- Four different forms of poems are free verse, haiku, concrete poems, and sonnets.

LESSON 1 RHYTHMS AND RHYME SCHEMES

Analyzing a poem to discover its patterns of rhythm and rhyme is called *scanning* a poem. Scanning is a useful step in recognizing similarities and differences among poems. Following are some concepts and terms needed for scanning poetry.

As you have learned, *rhythm* is defined as the pattern of stressed and unstressed syllables in a poem. Rhythms can sometimes be irregular, that is, without any particular arrangement of the stressed and unstressed syllables, as in this sentence:

/ ∪ ∪ / ∪/∪∪ ∪ / ∪   / /∪∪ /∪∪
Rhythms can be irregular, that is, without any particular
∪ / ∪
arrangement. . . .

Sometimes they're regular, as in this sentence:

/   ∪   ∪   /∪∪
Sometimes they're regular.

A regular rhythm repeats the same arrangement of stressed and unstressed syllables over and over. Another name for a regular rhythmic pattern is *meter*. Poems in English generally use four basic meters.

In English, it's fairly natural to speak in a meter that alternates single stressed and unstressed syllables. In poetry, that meter is given one name if the stressed syllable comes first (*trochee*), and another name if it comes second (*iamb*). You don't need to know the names of these meters to hear the differences between them:

/ ∪ / ∪ / ∪
Polly wants a cracker.   (*trochee*)

∪ / ∪ / ∪ /
The bird says just one thing.   (*iamb*)

Sometimes two unstressed syllables come between stressed syllables. Again, you hear a difference if the stressed syllable regularly comes first (*dactyl*) or if it comes second (*anapest*):

/ ∪ ∪ / ∪ ∪ / ∪ ∪
Everyone stared at the Cadillac.   (*dactyl*)

∪ ∪ / ∪ ∪ / ∪ ∪ /
I will pay for this car all my life. (*anapest*)

Meters are counted in *feet*. Each *foot* contains one stressed syllable. In the two samples you just read, each line has three stressed syllables. Therefore, each line has three feet.

Sometimes a poet establishes a certain rhythm in one foot and sticks to it throughout almost the entire poem. For an example, read these lines from the beginning of "An Elegy on the Death of a Mad Dog." The rhythm that Goldsmith has established here carries throughout the rest of the poem.

> ᴜ / ᴜ / ᴜ / ᴜ /
> Good people all, of every sort,
>   ᴜ / ᴜ / ᴜ /
>   Give ear unto my song;
> ᴜ / ᴜ / ᴜ / ᴜ /
> And if you find it wond'rous short,
>   ᴜ / ᴜ / ᴜ /
>   It cannot hold you long.

Without exception, each of these first four lines has perfect iambic feet. That means that each foot consists of an unaccented first syllable followed by an accented second syllable. The only variation in the lines is in the number of feet per line. Lines 1 and 3 have four feet each; Lines 2 and 4 have three feet each. This consistent pattern of iambic rhythm results in a sing-song effect.

Another characteristic that contributes to the sing-song effect is the pattern of rhyme on the short lines. Throughout the poem, the pattern in every stanza is *abab*. This pattern of rhyme is so consistent that it reinforces the metrical pattern.

The sing-song effect in "An Elegy on the Death of a Mad Dog" adds to the comic tone of the poem. A sing-song effect probably would not be as appropriate in a more serious poem, however. In more serious poems, poets generally establish a basic rhythmic pattern but then intentionally change it from time to time. In order to decide whether a poem's rhythm stays the same or changes, you must analyze several lines of the poem to see what appears most often.

EXERCISE ①

Reread the poems in Group 1. Then use what you have learned in this lesson to answer these questions:

1. Scan "The Eagle That Is Forgotten." What is its basic meter? Refer to the samples of meter in the lesson to find the name of that meter. How many feet occur in each line? What is the rhyme scheme or schemes of this poem?

2. Compare the metrical patterns of "The Eagle That Is Forgotten" and "When, in Disgrace with Fortune and Men's Eyes." How are the patterns different? How are they the same? Notice that the final line of "The Eagle That Is Forgotten" has a different number of feet than the other lines. Why did the poet introduce this variation? What is the effect of the extra beat?

Now check your answers with your teacher. Review this part of the lesson if you don't understand why an answer was incorrect.

WRITING ON YOUR OWN ①

In this exercise you will apply the rhythms that you just learned about to lines you write yourself. Follow these steps:

- In the lesson are samples of each of the four basic rhythms. Write an original sentence to illustrate each rhythm.
- Next, choose one of the four rhythms and one of these three rhyme schemes: *aba cbc, aab ccb, abc abc.* Write a six-line poem on any topic, following the patterns of rhythm and rhyme that you have chosen. Some variation in rhythm is acceptable, as long as one rhythm predominates.

LESSON ② FOUR FORMS OF POETRY

Some of the characteristics of poetry are these: (1) its appearance, or form, is different from other forms of writing; (2) it uses intense and striking language to present ideas and feelings; (3) it uses as few words as possible to express ideas and feelings; and (4) it emphasizes ideas and feelings through the effective uses of sound, including rhythmic patterns, rhymes, and other forms of repetition.

When poets use some of these different characteristics, they produce different forms of poetry. In this lesson you will look at four forms of poetry, each of which stresses a different characteristic:

Free verse is poetry that does not follow a particular pattern of rhythm or rhyme. Writers of free verse feel that they can express their ideas better without being tied down to a specific form or set of rules. Their language uses imagery of all sorts, and such sound techniques as alliteration, but it otherwise sounds like normal conversation. One of the earliest champions of free verse was Walt Whitman. Notice how this stanza of "Miracles" varies in length from line to line and from one metrical foot to the next.

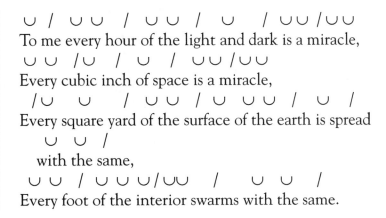

Haiku is a form of poetry adapted from Japanese poetry. It is an extremely short form of poetry that uses as few words as possible to describe an idea or experience. Every haiku consists of exactly 17 syllables arranged in 3 lines in a 5–7–5 pattern. Often, when a haiku is translated into English, it loses a syllable or so, as in the following haiku by Bashō. However, the poem's focus and message are clear in either language.

> Clouds now and then
> Giving men relief
> From moon-viewing.

Concrete poetry is poetry that has a special appearance. In a concrete poem, the poet arranges the words in a shape that suggests the subject of the poem. The poem may follow a definite pattern of rhythm and rhyme, it may be free verse, or it may lie somewhere in-between. For example, look back at May Swenson's "Unconscious Came a Beauty." Even before you read a word of the poem, you probably figured out from its shape that it was going to be about a butterfly.

A *sonnet* is a 14-line poem with fixed patterns of meter and rhyme. The most popular metrical pattern for a sonnet is *iambic pentameter,* which consists of five iambic feet ($\cup$ /) in each line. The two most common rhymes that appear in sonnets are the couplet and the quatrain. A *couplet* is 2 lines that end in rhyme: *aa.* A *quatrain* is 4 lines that usually follow one of these patterns: *abab, abba,* or *abcb.*

There are several different types of sonnets. Three of the most popular are Italian, French, and English sonnets—sometimes known as Shakespearean sonnets. The rhyme scheme in Shakespeare's sonnets has four parts: three quatrains and a closing couplet. The usual rhyme scheme is *abab cdcd efef gg.* For an example of this rhyme scheme, look at "When, in Disgrace with Fortune and Men's Eyes."

Notice how the development of the ideas is linked to the rhyme schemes within this sonnet. The first two quatrains present the speaker's problem: he feels like a failure, jealous of everyone else and not appreciating what he has. The third quatrain changes the mood as the speaker recognizes a solution to the problem: just thinking about his loved one makes him happy enough to sing. The final couplet settles the matter: as long as he has the love of the person to whom he is speaking, he doesn't need anything else.

EXERCISE (2)

Reread the poems in Group 2. Then use what you have learned in this lesson to answer these questions:

1. Compare the second haiku by Bashō with the requirements of haiku listed in this lesson. Does the form of this haiku vary from the standard number and arrangement of syllables? Does the content of this poem match the desired content of haiku poetry? Explain how the second haiku does or does not match the description.

2. What is suggested by the shape of the poem "Medicine"? How does it relate to the topic of the poem?

3. Scan the sonnet by William Wordsworth, "Composed upon Westminster Bridge, September 3, 1802." Does it follow iambic pentameter? If not, describe its rhythmic pattern. Identify the rhyme scheme. Discuss how the development of the poem's ideas corresponds to the rhyme scheme.

Now check your answers with your teacher. Review this part of the lesson if you don't understand why an answer was incorrect.

WRITING ON YOUR OWN (2)

Now that you recognize the essential characteristics of several forms of poetry, it's time to try your hand at some of them. Follow these steps:

- Review the two concrete poems in this unit. Then choose an object that can be represented in an easily recognizable shape, such as a tree, a flower, a boat, or a star. Draw up a list of words and phrases that describe your chosen object. Next, arrange those words and phrases so that they resemble the shape of the object. Use any of the following suggestions if you need to improve the poem's shape: 1) to make lines longer, add describing words or simply stretch out the letters; 2) to make lines shorter, write your words in narrow, crowded letters or divide words onto two lines; 3) if you need to include more than one idea on a line, separate the ideas with dashes to make them clearer.

- When you finish your poem, ask a classmate to guess what the poem is about by identifying its shape before reading it. Then have your classmate read the poem and report whether its content matched his or her expectations.

- Using some of the words or phrases from your concrete poem, write a second poem on the same subject. This time, however, write your poem in either free verse or haiku form. If you write in free verse, include some form of repetition—of letters, or words, or both.

DISCUSSION GUIDES

1. In "The Eagle That Is Forgotten," Vachel Lindsay honors a man who took a stand for justice to workers at a time when labor and business were practically at war. Research the labor problems at the turn of the century, the Haymarket Riot and other demonstrations, and John P. Altgeld. Were there other leaders like Altgeld who contributed to the easing of the conflict? Report your findings to the class.

2. In "Miracles," Walt Whitman lists some of his favorite activities and scenes. Would you have put together the same list? With a small group, rewrite lines 3 through 14 of this poem, inserting new activities and scenes that the group agrees on. Try to vary your line lengths, just as Whitman's original lines are varied. Share your completed revision with the rest of the class.

3. Review the poems that you liked best in the other units. Were they mostly in free verse, mostly in more traditional forms, or pretty well split between the two types? If you were to go to the library in search of additional poems to read on your own, would you look for poems in free verse, traditional poems, or both? Why? If you were to become a professional poet, which type of poem would you most likely produce? Why? Take a poll of your class to discover whether one kind of poetry is generally preferred, and if so, which type is preferred and why.

4. Which three poems in this unit did you like best? List them in your order of preference. Next, focus on your first-ranked poem and decide which of its characteristics helped make it your favorite. Write a short nominating speech for your poem, explaining why it should be elected Best Poem of Unit 6. Read your speech to the class and invite others to read their speeches. Then take a vote on the Best Poem of Unit 6.

WRITE A SONNET

In this unit you have studied metrical patterns and other characteristics that give form to poems. You have written sentences illustrating metrical patterns, a short traditional poem, and two poems in nontraditional forms. In this exercise you will write a longer poem in the traditional form of a sonnet.

Follow these steps to write your sonnet. If you have questions about the writing process, refer to Using the Writing Process on page 232.

- Assemble and review the work you did for all the writing exercises in this unit: 1) two lists of well-known phrases and sentences, marked to show their rhythmic patterns; 2) samples illustrating all four metrical patterns; 3) a six-line poem using patterns of rhythm and rhyme; 4) a concrete poem and either a haiku or a free-verse poem about the same topic.
- With a group of classmates, review the characteristics of an English sonnet described in this unit. Then reread the sonnets by Shakespeare and Wordsworth and study these examples. Then work together and write a group sonnet.
- The form of your sonnet can match the English format, or you can add variations. Even if you use variations, however, your sonnet should show a development in thought. Choose a topic that can be developed in two stages, and decide how your pattern of rhyme will give a clue to the movement from one stage to the next. For example, the first part of your sonnet could describe a problem and the second part could describe the solution, or the first part could describe a scene or event and the second part could describe your feelings about it.
- Decide on the metrical pattern you will use in your sonnet. Most sonnets are written in iambic pentameter. If, in the earlier exercises, some of you found it easier to write in a different meter, however, you might want to discuss using that meter instead. Each line should have no fewer than three feet of whatever meter you choose.

- As you write your sonnet, keep in mind all that you have learned about speakers, sensory details, figurative language, and sound techniques. Try to use as many of these techniques as possible.
- Set the sonnet aside for at least a day. Then get back together with your group and have a member or members read the sonnet aloud. Discuss any revisions that you think will improve its form or meaning.
- When you have finished revising the sonnet, take turns proofreading it for spelling, grammar, and formatting errors. Then have another group member make a final copy. Share your sonnet with the rest of the class. If possible, make enough photocopies of the sonnet so that each group member can store a copy in his or her writing portfolio.

Author's Purpose

INTRODUCTION

ABOUT THE LESSONS

Why do people write poems? The answers to that question are as varied as the poets themselves. Poets may write to celebrate special occasions, to share personal feelings, to describe significant experiences, or simply to enjoy the sound of language. Many poets write to explain a certain point of view or to persuade readers to adopt a particular way of thinking or acting.

The poems in this unit are divided into three groups. Group 1 contains examples of poems with clear purposes and themes. Group 2 features poems containing speakers with unmistakable tones, or attitudes. Group 3 contains poems that can be used to help you analyze and evaluate poetry from your own point of view.

WRITING: DISCUSSING A POEM

At the end of this unit you will write a short essay in which you evaluate a particular poem. Follow these steps to start thinking about some poems you could evaluate:

- Review the first six units of this book, listing one or two poems from each unit that appeal to you most.
- You chose each of the poems on your list for a reason. Perhaps it was the surprising figurative language or the conversational tone of the speaker. Maybe you enjoy the precision of the haiku form or the exuberance of a particular rhythm. Think about why you chose each poem and record your reasons beside each title.
- Save your work to use in later writing exercises.

ABOUT THIS POET

Pat Mora (1942–) was born in El Paso, Texas, near the Mexican border. Her grandparents had all come to the United States from Mexico. Growing up, Mora spoke Spanish in her home but she didn't always want her friends to know that. Now she is proudly bilingual and wants to encourage children of Hispanic background to treasure their heritage.

Mora received her bachelor's degree from Texas Western College and her master's degree from the University of Texas at El Paso. She was a high school and college teacher for several years but in 1981 began her writing career in earnest. By 1984 she had won several prizes for her first collections of poetry, *Chants* and *Borders*. Like much of her work, these collections focus on the Southwest and the Mexican-American culture that she loves. From 1983 to 1984, Mora was the host of a radio show called *Voices: The Mexican-American in Perspective* on National Public Radio.

Through her poetry, Mora has become a voice for both women and Mexican Americans. She stresses the importance of respecting all of our cultural legacies. She says, "I take pride in being a Hispanic writer. I will continue to write and to struggle to say what no other writer can say in quite the same way."

AS YOU READ

As you read each of the poems in this unit, ask yourself the following questions:

- Why has the poet written this poem? What message does the poem communicate?
- What is the speaker's attitude toward the subject of the poem? toward the audience? toward himself or herself? How do these attitudes support the poem's message, or theme?
- What are the most important elements in this poem? What has the poet done particularly well? Considering what you usually look for in poetry, what—if anything—do you think is missing from this poem?

Ozymandias

by Percy Bysshe Shelley

ABOUT THE SELECTION Percy Bysshe Shelley (1792–1822) was born into a wealthy family in England. His extreme intellectual views caused him to be expelled from Oxford University. During his brief and turbulent life, he shocked his countrymen with his opinions on love, marriage, and politics. His second wife was Mary Wollstonecraft Godwin, who wrote the novel *Frankenstein.* Shelley died at the age of 30 in a boating accident off the coast of Italy. In this poem, he ponders the fleeting nature of fame.

I met a traveler from an antique land
Who said: Two vast and trunkless legs of stone
Stand in the desert. Near them, on the sand,
Half sunk, a shattered visage[1] lies, whose frown,
And wrinkled lip, and sneer of cold command,
Tell that its sculptor well those passions read
Which yet survive, stamped on these lifeless things,
The hand that mocked them and the heart that fed;
And on the pedestal these words appear:
"My name is Ozymandias, king of kings:
Look on my works, ye Mighty, and despair!"
Nothing beside remains. Round the decay
Of that colossal wreck, boundless and bare
The lone and level sands stretch far away.

---

[1] face

Concord Hymn

Sung at the completion of the Battle Monument, July 4, 1837

by Ralph Waldo Emerson

ABOUT THE SELECTION

Ralph Waldo Emerson (1803–1882) was born in Boston and lived his whole life near that city. After working as a school-teacher and Unitarian minister for several years, he turned to writing and lecturing. Emerson wrote the following poem to be read at the dedication of a memorial to the militia who faced the British army at the Concord Bridge in Massachusetts.

By the rude bridge that arched the flood,
    Their flag to April's breeze unfurled,
Here once the embattled farmers stood
    And fired the shot heard round the world.

The foe long since in silence slept;
    Alike the conqueror silent sleeps;
And Time the ruined bridge has swept
    Down the dark stream which seaward creeps.

On this green bank, by this soft stream,
    We set to-day a votive[1] stone;
That memory may their deed redeem,
    When, like our sires,[2] our sons are gone.

Spirit, that made those heroes dare
    To die, and leave their children free,
Bid Time and Nature gently spare
    The shaft we raise to them and thee.

----

[1] promised or done by a vow

[2] fathers

Legal Alien

by Pat Mora

ABOUT THE SELECTION

Pat Mora (1942–   ) works enthusiastically to preserve the Mexican-American culture. In this poem, she describes the feelings of Mexican Americans as they interact with both of their cultures. For more information about Mora, see About This Poet at the beginning of this unit.

Bi-lingual, Bi-cultural,
able to slip from "How's life?"
to *"Me'stan volviendo loca,"*[1]
able to sit in a paneled office
drafting memos in smooth English,
able to order in fluent Spanish
at a Mexican restaurant,
American but hyphenated,
viewed by Anglos as perhaps exotic,
perhaps inferior, definitely different,
viewed by Mexicans as alien,
(their eyes say, "You may speak
Spanish but you're not like me")
an American to Mexicans
a Mexican to Americans
a handy token
sliding back and forth
between the fringes of both worlds
by smiling
by masking the discomfort
of being pre-judged
Bi-laterally.[2]

---

[1] They're driving me crazy. (Spanish)

[2] on two sides

GROUP 2

One Perfect Rose

by Dorothy Parker

ABOUT THE SELECTION

Dorothy Parker (1893–1967) was known for both her writing and her biting wit. Parker wrote poetry and short stories and was a drama critic in New York City. Along with other writers and critics, including humorist Robert Benchley and playwright Robert Sherwood, Parker participated in famous, informal lunchtime discussions at the Algonquin Hotel. Parker's sense of humor is reflected in her books of poetry, which include *Enough Rope, Death and Taxes,* and *Not So Deep as a Well.* Her humor also is evident in the following poem.

A single flow'r he sent me, since we met.
    All tenderly his messenger he chose;
Deep-hearted, pure, with scented dew still wet—
    One perfect rose.

I knew the language of the floweret;
    "My fragile leaves," it said, "his heart enclose."
Love long has taken for his amulet[1]
    One perfect rose.

Why is it no one ever sent me yet
    One perfect limousine, do you suppose?
Ah no, it's always just my luck to get
    One perfect rose.

---

[1] a good-luck charm

The Lesson of the Moth

by Don Marquis

ABOUT THE SELECTION

Don Marquis (1878–1937) was best known for his humorous *New York Evening Sun* columns. In them, he spoke as a cockroach named archy and an alley cat named mehitabel who used Marquis' typewriter at night. (The animals couldn't reach the type-writer key that prints capital letters.) The following poem is one of the messages that archy left for his "boss" to read one morning.

i was talking to a moth
the other evening
he was trying to break into
an electric light bulb
and fry himself on the wires

why do you fellows
pull this stunt i asked him
because it is the conventional
thing for moths or why
if that had been an uncovered
candle instead of an electric
light bulb you would
now be a small unsightly cinder
have you no sense
plenty of it he answered
but at times we get tired
of using it
we get bored with the routine
and crave beauty
and excitement

fire is beautiful
and we know that if we get
too close it will kill us
but what does that matter
it is better to be happy
for a moment
and be burned up with beauty
than to live a long time
and be bored all the while
so we wad all our life up
into one little roll
and then we shoot the roll
that is what life is for
it is better to be a part of beauty
for one instant and then cease to
exist than to exist forever
and never be a part of beauty
our attitude toward life
is come easy go easy
we are like human beings
used to be before they became
too civilized to enjoy themselves

and before i could argue him
out of his philosophy
he went and immolated[1] himself
on a patent cigar lighter
i do not agree with him
myself i would rather have
half the happiness and twice
the longevity

but at the same time i wish
there was something i wanted
as badly as he wanted to fry himself

                          archy

---

[1] died by fire, sometimes said of a sacrificial death

George Gray

by Edgar Lee Masters

ABOUT THE SELECTION

Edgar Lee Masters (1868–1950) was born in Garnett, Kansas. For many years, he was a lawyer in Chicago while he wrote poetry on the side. In 1915 he published *Spoon River Anthology,* a collection of poems in which the speakers are supposedly the dead citizens of a small town named Spoon River. In these poems the speakers comment on their lives—their wasted opportunities, their sorrows, and their joys. The book was an immediate success with the public. Although Masters went on to quit his job as an attorney and write other poetry, his later work was not as successful as *Spoon River Anthology,* from which this poem is taken.

I have studied many times
The marble which was chiseled for me—
A boat with a furled[1] sail at rest in a harbor.
In truth it pictures not my destination
But my life.
For love was offered me and I shrank from its disillusionment;
Sorrow knocked at my door, but I was afraid;
Ambition called to me, but I dreaded the chances.
Yet all the while I hungered for meaning in my life.
And now I know that we must lift the sail
And catch the winds of destiny
Wherever they drive the boat.
To put meaning in one's life may end in madness,
But life without meaning is the torture
Of restlessness and vague desire—
It is a boat longing for the sea and yet afraid.

---

[1]wrapped close to the mast

The Man from Washington

by James Welch

ABOUT THE SELECTION

James Welch (1940–   ) was born in Browning, Montana. His parents belonged to the Blackfeet and Gros Ventre tribes. He attended reservation schools and schools in Minneapolis, Minnesota, before graduating from the University of Montana. While writing poetry and novels, Welch has earned his living as a laborer, firefighter, and counselor. One of his most recent writing efforts is a nonfiction book entitled *Killing Custer: The Battle of Little Bighorn and the Fate of the Plains Indians.* As you read "The Man from Washington," you will be struck by the attitude of the speaker in this poem, which was written from a Native American's point of view.

The end came easy for most of us.
Packed away in our crude beginnings
in some far corner of a flat world,
we didn't expect much more
than firewood and buffalo robes
to keep us warm. The man came down,
a slouching dwarf with rainwater eyes,
and spoke to us. He promised
that life would go on as usual,
that treaties would be signed, and everyone—
man, woman and child—would be inoculated[1]
against a world in which we had no part,
a world of money, promise and disease.

---

[1] vaccinated in order to be protected against disease

The Listeners

by Walter de la Mare

ABOUT THE SELECTION

Walter de la Mare (1873–1956) was born in Kent, England. For financial reasons, he left school when he was a teenager and took a job as a bookkeeper for Standard Oil in England. He held that position for the next 18 years. He always thought of himself as a poet, and in middle age he began writing full-time. Although he also wrote novels and edited anthologies, he is best known for his imaginative poetry. His book *The Listeners and Other Poems,* from which this poem is taken, was his first book to become popular with the public.

"Is there anybody there?" said the Traveler,
   Knocking on the moonlit door;
And his horse in the silence champed the grasses
   Of the forest's ferny floor:
And a bird flew up out of the turret,[1]
   Above the Traveler's head:
And he smote upon the door again a second time;
   "Is there anybody there?" he said.
But no one descended to the Traveler;
   No head from the leaf-fringed sill
Leaned over and looked into his gray eyes,
   Where he stood perplexed and still.
But only a host of phantom listeners
   That dwelt in the lone house then

---

[1] little tower

Stood listening in the quiet of the moonlight
    To that voice from the world of men:
Stood thronging[2] the faint moonbeams on the dark stair,
    That goes down to the empty hall,
Hearkening[3] in an air stirred and shaken
    By the lonely Traveler's call.
And he felt in his heart their strangeness,
    Their stillness answering his cry,
While his horse moved, cropping the dark turf,
    'Neath the starred and leafy sky;
For he suddenly smote on the door, even
    Louder, and lifted his head:—
"Tell them I came, and no one answered,
    That I kept my word," he said.
Never the least stir made the listeners,
    Though every word he spake
Fell echoing through the shadowiness of the still house
    From the one man left awake:
Ay, they heard his foot upon the stirrup,
    And the sound of iron on stone,
And how the silence surged softly backward,
    When the plunging hoofs were gone.

---

[2] crowding together

[3] listening

Water Picture

by May Swenson

ABOUT THE SELECTION

May Swenson (1919–1989) was known for her precise observations of nature and her unusual way of looking at everyday objects. She was born in Logan, Utah, and later graduated from Utah State University. After college, she soon moved to New York City, where she lived for most of her life. Swenson was the recipient of numerous awards for her poetry and was guest lecturer at dozens of universities across the United States. She published 12 volumes of poetry and contributed her poems to several anthologies. Her unique observational and descriptive skills are evident in the following poem.

In the pond in the park
all things are doubled:
Long buildings hang and
wriggle gently. Chimneys
are bent legs bouncing
on clouds below. A flag
wags like a fishhook
down there in the sky.

The arched stone bridge
is an eye, with underlid
in the water. In its lens
dip crinkled heads with hats
that don't fall off. Dogs go by,
barking on their backs.
A baby, taken to feed the
ducks, dangles upside-down,
a pink balloon for a buoy.

Treetops deploy a haze of
cherry bloom for roots,
where birds coast belly-up
in the glass bowl of a hill;
from its bottom a bunch
of peanut-munching children
is suspended by their
sneakers, waveringly.

A swan, with twin necks
forming the figure three,
steers between two dimpled
towers doubled. Fondly
hissing, she kisses herself,
and all the scene is troubled:
water-windows splinter,
tree-limbs tangle, the bridge
folds like a fan.

UNDERSTANDING THE POEMS

Record your answers to these questions in your personal literature notebook. Follow the directions for each group.

GROUP 1   Reread the poems in Group 1 to complete these sentences.

Reviewing the Selection

1. In "Concord Hymn" the speaker says that the actual bridge where the farmers made their stand has now
   a. become a national treasure.
   b. been washed out to sea.
   c. been destroyed by the foe.
   d. been spared by Time and Nature.

2. The statue of Ozymandias is located
   a. in the middle of a lonely desert.
   b. near a city filled with antiques.
   c. beside the Pyramids in Egypt.
   d. near the wreck of a sunken ship.

Interpreting the Selection

3. The speaker in "Legal Alien" expresses all these feelings *except*
   a. pride in being able to function in two cultures.
   b. resentment at not being accepted in the United States or Mexico.
   c. disappointment at not feeling totally comfortable in either culture.
   d. a feeling of superiority over both American and Mexican cultures.

Recognizing How Words Are Used

4. In "Ozymandias" the line "The lone and level sands stretch far away" has this number of strong beats, or accented syllables:
   a. four.
   b. five.
   c. eight.
   d. ten.

Appreciating Poetry   **5.** When the speaker says that the shot fired at Concord was "heard round the world," he or she means that

    a. the gun that fired the shot was louder than any gun in the world.

    b. the war that began here affected countries around the world.

    c. the shot really was loud and could be heard around the world.

    d. a strange phenomenon caused the shot to travel around the world.

GROUP 2   Reread the poems in Group 2 to complete these sentences.

Reviewing the   **6.** The speaker in "The Lesson of the Moth" is puzzled by the
Selection   moth's action of

    a. eating wool and other cloths.

    b. smoking cigars.

    c. deliberately flying into a flame.

    d. attempting difficult flying stunts.

7. On the tombstone of the speaker in "George Gray," you would find a carving of

    a. a sailboat with its sails folded against the mast.

    b. a weeping willow tree bending low.

    c. a man knocking at a door.

    d. the crashing waves of an ocean.

Interpreting the   **8.** "The Man from Washington" who makes a series of
Selection   promises to Native Americans is probably

    a. the President of the United States.

    b. a local merchant who wants to sell goods to the tribes.

    c. an anonymous government worker.

    d. a man from the state of Washington.

Recognizing How Words Are Used

9. The only poem in Group 2 that contains rhyme is
    a. "The Lesson of the Moth."
    b. "The Man from Washington."
    c. "George Gray."
    d. "One Perfect Rose."

Appreciating Poetry

10. The speaker in "One Perfect Rose" is most likely a
    a. middle-aged woman.
    b. little girl.
    c. woman who is deeply in love.
    d. woman who runs a flower shop.

GROUP 3   Reread the poems in Group 3 to complete these sentences.

Reviewing the Selection

11. The traveler in "The Listeners" knocks at the door because
    a. he wants to help the house's inhabitants escape.
    b. he wants a place to spend the night.
    c. he promised unknown persons that he would stop by.
    d. the ghosts inside have commanded him to do so.

12. In "Water Picture" the speaker sees all of these objects reflected in the water except
    a. an arched stone bridge.
    b. a baby who came to feed the ducks.
    c. a waving flag.
    d. girls jumping rope.

Interpreting the Selection

13. When the speaker in "Water Picture" says that the swan kisses herself, this means that the swan has
    a. touched its beak to its reflection in the water.
    b. stroked its own feathers.
    c. nuzzled its babies.
    d. touched another swan on the beak.

Recognizing How **14.** In "The Listeners" the "sound of iron on stone" refers to the
Words Are Used   sound of

      a. the iron knocker hitting the stone door.
      b. a stone falling from the house onto the traveler's stirrups.
      c. the barrel of a shotgun set upon the house's window sill.
      d. the horse's iron-shod hoofs against the stone road by the
         house.

Appreciating Poetry **15.** The mood of "The Listeners" could be described as

      a. resentful.
      b. mysterious.
      c. hopeful.
      d. practical.

Now check your answers with your teacher. Study the
questions you answered incorrectly. What types of questions
were they? Talk with your teacher about ways to work on
those skills.

UNIT 7 LESSONS

Author's Purpose

Before most writers put a word down on paper, they usually are already aware of their reason, or purpose, for writing. For example, students may write test essays to prove that they have mastered a concept, lawyers may draft their closing arguments to persuade juries to rule in their clients' favor, and biographers may want to tell about people's lives so that readers can understand those people better. Even writers who write personal pieces that they don't expect others to see have a purpose: they need to express or clarify their feelings.

Poems are written for a variety of reasons. Poets' purposes for writing affect both what they say and how they say it. When you are trying to understand a particular poem, it is useful to try to discover the poet's purpose for writing it.

Perhaps a poet's purpose is to share with readers an insight about life that he or she has learned. This insight is called a *theme*. In most writing, but especially in poetry, the theme is not always obvious. It often takes careful rereading to understand a poet's message. One clue to the theme is the *tone*, or attitude, of the poem's speaker.

In the following lessons you will examine author's purpose, paying special attention to these ideas:

- Because the theme of a poem usually is not obvious, the key to unlocking the theme lies in careful reading and rereading.
- A poet conveys the theme through the persona, or voice, of the speaker. Readers can use the speaker's tone to discover a poem's theme and purpose.
- To evaluate any poem fairly, you must analyze it part by part. Then you can decide if the poet has accomplished his or her purpose. Your evaluation will be both objective and subjective.

LESSON ①   AUTHOR'S PURPOSE AND THEME

Like any other type of writing, television comedies and dramas have *themes*, or general messages about life, that they hope to convey to viewers. When television producers are preparing to air new programs, they are faced with an important decision: what should be used as the theme song? They want the theme song—which will be played at the beginning and the end of the show—to somehow reflect the theme that the series is based on. For example, a light, family-oriented comedy might choose a catchy tune performed by a happy singer to convey the idea that this old world is a pretty nice place after all. A science-fiction show might choose an otherworldly, wordless song to suggest the theme that mysterious wonders are all around us in the universe. An adventure series might choose a loud, fast piece featuring screaming guitars or blaring trumpets to show that true happiness comes from taking risks and living boldly. A theme song prepares viewers for the stories that are to come and gives hints about the message that the programs will try to convey each week. Then, as each show unfolds, the theme is explained more specifically through the events that take place.

In a television series, the writers have many opportunities to expand upon their central themes. However, in a poem the writer must communicate the theme in just a few words. For that reason, poets pack as much meaning as possible into each word and phrase—and even the punctuation. As mentioned earlier, to understand the theme of a poem often requires several readings. The first time through, the surface meaning may be obvious. With the next reading, however, you may notice ideas and images that got by you the first time. During each rereading, you'll probably see even deeper meanings.

For example, even the theme of a simple poem like "Concord Hymn" becomes clearer with rereading. The first time they read this poem, most readers probably concentrate on the noble image of farmers standing by the stream protecting their freedom and "the shot heard round the world." Only a few readers will focus on and remember the words of the second stanza:

> The foe long since in silence slept;
>   Alike the conqueror silent sleeps;
> And Time the ruined bridge has swept
>   Down the dark stream which seaward creeps.

One underlying theme of the poem may be that acts of bravery are too often forgotten by those who come later. Emerson's purpose in writing this poem was to celebrate the effort to keep the memory of the farmers' courage alive so it will inspire others to act in a similar way.

The theme of "Legal Alien" by Pat Mora also becomes clearer after you reread the poem. On the first reading, you may sense the speaker's distress at not belonging fully to either of his or her cultures. During later rereadings, however, you may notice the use of hyphens where you normally don't see them:

> Bi-lingual, Bi-cultural,
> able to slip from "How's life?"
> to "Me'stan volviendo loca,"
> able to sit in a paneled office
> drafting memos in smooth English,
> able to order in fluent Spanish
> at a Mexican restaurant,
> American but hyphenated, . . .
> a handy token
> sliding back and forth
> between the fringes of both worlds
> by smiling
> by masking the discomfort
> of being pre-judged
> Bi-laterally.

Why does the speaker repeatedly use hyphens? It could be that hyphenated words are words that combine two ideas but resist being swallowed into a single word. The parts of hyphenated words maintain their separateness, just as the speaker seems to want to maintain both his or her Mexican and American identities. Does the emphasis on hyphens mean that the speaker sees no way out of the dilemma if he or she doesn't want to be absorbed into one or the other culture? Perhaps one theme of the poem could be that the discomfort of not fully belonging is unavoidable for now.

EXERCISE ①

Reread "Ozymandias" by Percy Bysshe Shelley. Then use what you have learned in this lesson to answer these questions:

1. What has happened to the statue of Ozymandias over the years? What words were inscribed in the pedestal long ago? Explain why the words make the fate of the statue seem ironic—that is, the opposite of what Ozymandias expected.

2. What message does this poem convey regarding people who pride themselves on their power and importance?

Now check your answers with your teacher. Review this part of the lesson if you don't understand why an answer was incorrect.

 ## WRITING ON YOUR OWN ①

In this exercise you will identify the themes from several poems and will create a matching game involving those themes. Follow these steps:

- Throughout this book you have read many poems with strong themes. Look through the book and find five poems that you feel have the clearest or strongest themes.
- Divide a sheet of paper into two columns. In the left-hand column, list the titles of the poems. In the right-hand column—in an order that is different from the order of the titles—write five short statements to explain each theme. Since this is for a matching activity, make sure that the themes are not directly across from their corresponding titles.
- Give your paper to a classmate and have him or her match the titles and themes. When he or she is finished, discuss whether or not you both agree on the themes you have dentified.

LESSON ②

TONE AND THEME

The poems in Group 2 feature a variety of speakers—a cockroach, a disillusioned lover, an angry Native American, and a deceased citizen of a small town. Although the poems have different speakers and address different subjects, they all have one thing in common: Each of their speakers has a distinct and conspicuous *tone*, or attitude.

In "The Lesson of the Moth" archy the cockroach approaches his topic in an offhanded way at first, idly inquiring why the moth continually chooses to "pull the stunt" of flying toward a light in spite of the danger. The speaker's tone is communicated through his conversational way of speaking and the everyday, informal words he uses:

> i was talking to a moth
> the other evening
> he was trying to break into
> an electric light bulb
> and fry himself on the wires

why do you fellows
pull this stunt i asked him

The speaker acts as if the conversation were unimportant, certainly not worth dignifying with formal speech, and instead uses words and phrases such as "fry himself on the wires," "fellows," and "pull this stunt." However, the tone becomes more thoughtful and respectful by the end of the poem:

i do not agree with him
myself i would rather have
half the happiness and twice
the longevity

but at the same time i wish
there was something i wanted
as badly as he wanted to fry himself

The tone has changed slightly, and we understand that the speaker—even though he still can't agree with the moth's philosophy—takes it seriously. The speaker has found that his encounter with the moth has made him examine his own philosophy of life.

The speaker's attitude in "One Perfect Rose" doesn't actually change, but our understanding of her tone increases from the beginning of the poem to its conclusion. The poem begins with an expression of what seems to be the speaker's sincere gratitude for a romantic gift:

A single flow'r he sent me, since we met.
　　　All tenderly his messenger he chose;
Deep-hearted, pure, with scented dew still wet—
　　　One perfect rose.

The words the speaker has chosen—for example, the poetic spelling of *flower* as *flow'r* and the lovely image of a rose with "scented dew still wet"—lead readers to believe that the speaker genuinely appreciates the simple gift. However, the last stanza reveals the truth: the speaker would rather have a limousine. She was being sarcastic in the first two stanzas. When you reread them in light of this fact, you understand that the speaker's attitude hasn't really changed; you just finally get the joke.

The tone of the speaker in "The Man from Washington" is anything but light and humorous. His or her anger and resentment permeate the poem through the poet's words, details, and images. The speaker seems to be disappointed in his or her people for being vulnerable ("Packed away in our crude beginnings/in some corner of a flat world/we didn't expect much more/than firewood and buffalo robes/to keep us warm."). He or she is sarcastic and sorrowful about the way their lives have worked out since the lies were told to them:

> . . . He promised
> that life would go on as usual,
> that treaties would be signed, and everyone—
> man, woman and child— would be inoculated
> against a world in which we had no part,
> a world of money, promise and disease.

But the speaker saves the most damning evidence of his feelings for the repulsive image of the government man: "a slouching dwarf with rainwater eyes." The speaker's outraged tone reinforces the poem's theme that Native Americans were taken advantage of and treated dishonestly by the government.

EXERCISE ②

Reread "George Gray." Then use what you have learned in this lesson to answer these questions:

1. How would you describe the tone of "George Gray"? Consider the speaker's feelings as he reflects upon his life.

2. What is the theme of the poem—that is, what lesson about life does the poet wish to share? How does the speaker's tone help to convey the theme?

Now check your answers with your teacher. Review this part of the lesson if you don't understand why an answer was incorrect.

WRITING ON YOUR OWN ②

In this lesson you have learned that a poet creates a tone by using particular words, details, and images. In this lesson you will analyze a particular poem with regard to those techniques. Follow these steps:

- In the first writing exercise in this unit you made a list of your favorite poems from this book. Look over that list and find a poem in which the speaker conveys a strong tone. Write the poem's title on the top of a sheet of paper. Below the title, write a word or phrase that identifies the speaker's tone—for example: tender, angry, elated, regretful, or critical.
- Now divide the paper into three columns. Label the first column *Words,* the second column *Details,* and the third column *Images.*
- Reread the poem several times. Decide which words, details, and images contribute most strongly to the tone. Record them in the appropriate columns.

LESSON ③ ANALYZING AND EVALUATING A POEM

There are people whose job it is to review and evaluate other people's writing. They are usually well-qualified for the task, having studied literature for years and applied essential writing techniques themselves. In their study of literature, they have read a great number of short stories, novels, and poems and have become experienced in noticing the characteristics that set good literature apart from merely adequate or even inferior work. The chances are good that only a few people who read this book will become professional literary critics. Even so, as you go through life you probably will want to be able to choose good literature to read for enjoyment. Reading a good poem can expand your thinking and can help you see the world from different viewpoints at different stages in your life. For these reasons, although you may not be qualified to judge poetry as well as a professional critic can, you should know how to discuss and evaluate poems intelligently. What you have learned so far in this book will help you with that task.

What makes a good poem? For personal reading, you can create your own standards to answer that question. However, to be fair, you should develop a set of standards that help you evaluate many elements of a poem. As you have studied each of the units in this book, you have learned about these elements of poetry: speaker, imagery, sound devices, figurative language, form, and author's purpose. You have had experience in analyzing elements such as rhyme scheme, meter, theme, and tone. By now you understand that a good poem is a combination of many of these elements. No poem is outstanding in all elements, but every good poem is strong in several of them.

To evaluate a poem, therefore, you have to examine it element by element, concentrating on its strengths. For example, one poem may excel in its use of vivid sensory images and concrete language to communicate an unusual theme. It would be foolish to ignore those strengths when you evaluate the poem just because you may not sympathize with its speaker. At the same time, you need to be aware that your own preferences will affect your overall judgment of the poem. The best evaluations of poetry combine an objective analysis of how well the poem accomplishes its purpose and a statement of your subjective opinion.

Read the following evaluation of "Water Picture." On which elements of poetry does the writer concentrate? At which points is it obvious that the discussion reflects one person's subjective opinion? Notice how the essay begins with a summary of what the poem is about.

"Water Picture" by May Swenson recreates the experience of being at a pond in the park on a beautiful spring day. As the speaker looks into the reflections in the water, he or she sees surrounding objects, including buildings, a flag, a bridge, dogs, a baby, a balloon, blooming trees, and a swan. This is not an ordinary scene, however, because everything looks upside down. The strange perspective makes everyday objects seem unusual and surprising. The poem ends when the swan touches the surface of the pond with its beak and disturbs the water's stillness.

This poem does an excellent job of painting a picture with words, just as an artist paints a picture with paints. Like a painter, the poet does more than just recreate reality. She creates a dreamlike mood with sensory details such as "A flag/wags like a fishhook/down there in the sky," and "Dogs go by,/barking on their backs." She uses concrete language such as "peanut-munching children," but then she surprises you with her further description of the children as "suspended by their sneakers, waveringly." The sensory details and images build up so clearly that you feel that you could paint a real picture of this scene yourself, using paints on a canvas.

Swenson has chosen exact words to recreate the scene. She doesn't simply say, "When you look into the water, you see tall buildings standing by the pond. They appear to be upside down." Instead, she uses exact, specific words: "Long buildings hang and wriggle gently."

To show that the buildings are upside down, she uses the word *long* instead of *tall*, and *hang* instead of *stand*. To describe how their reflections move with the water, she uses the word *wriggle*. She has carefully chosen all of these words to not only describe the scene but to express the mood of the poem.

Swenson's effective use of sensory details, concrete language, and exact words to describe the scene and create the mood make this poem one of my favorites. I am sure that I will think of it the next time I visit the pond at my local park.

The writer of this evaluation concentrates on the strong use of imagery, sensory details, and mood in the poem. Note that the writer provides supporting evidence from the poem as well as reasons for his or her opinion. He or she peppers the essay with subjective words such as *excellent*, *effective*, *carefully*, and *my favorite* to not only report on the poem but to offer an opinion about it as well.

EXERCISE ③

Reread the poems in Group 3 and then use what you have learned in this lesson to answer these questions:

1. If you were going to write an evaluation of "The Listeners," on which elements of poetry would you concentrate—imagery; sensory details and concrete language; the speaker; rhythm, rhyme, and other sound devices; figurative language; mood; or tone? Choose at least two of these elements and explain why you feel that they are effective or ineffective in this poem.

2. Which one of your friends or family members do you think would enjoy reading "The Listeners"? Who do you think might enjoy "Water Picture"? Explain the reasons you chose those individuals. What characteristic(s) of each poem led you to match it with each person?

Now check your answers with your teacher. Review this part of the lesson if you don't understand why an answer was incorrect.

 WRITING ON YOUR OWN ③

In a previous writing exercise you listed poems that you enjoy from each unit. Now you will concentrate on one poem in greater detail. Follow these steps:

- Review your list of favorite poems. For some poems, it may be difficult to explain exactly what you like about them. For other poems, however, you probably can identify several reasons they made your list. Choose the one poem about which you feel you have the most to say.
- Next, make notes about how the poet handles each of the following poetic elements. (For example, if your chosen poem were "The Listeners," under *mood* you might write, "Description of the spirits inside the house creates a mysterious mood.") Here are the elements:
  a. speaker
  b. imagery and concrete language
  c. sound devices
  d. figurative language
  e. mood
  f. form
  g. theme
  h. tone
- Don't be surprised if some elements are easier to fill in than others.

DISCUSSION GUIDES

1. How much do you know about the battle that took place at the Concord Bridge in 1775? What events led up to it, and how did it change American history? How many colonists participated in the battle? Was anyone killed or wounded? Do some research on this particular battle and summarize your findings in a short report that you present to the rest of the class.

2. With a small group of classmates, create an anthology of your favorite poems. Each member of the group should find at least five poems to be considered for possible inclusion. Choose poems from this book or from other collections. When you find a poem that you feel should be included, read it aloud to the group for general approval. Explain what you like best about the poem and then decide together whether or not to include it. After all the poems have been chosen, decide on the order in which they should appear. Can you find a connection among the poems, for example, similar themes or forms? Are two or more of the poems written by the same person? Finally, assemble all of your chosen poems and arrange them in order in a folder or booklet to be shared with others.

3. At the end of Unit 1 of this book, your class developed a questionnaire about your attitudes toward poetry. Now that your study of poetry is nearing its end, take a few moments to answer the survey questions again. After the results are tabulated, see if your class's attitudes toward poetry have changed.

EVALUATE A POEM

In this unit you have examined the role of theme and tone in accomplishing the author's purpose. You also have begun thinking about how to discuss and evaluate poems. Now it is time to write a short essay evaluating a particular poem.

Follow these steps to write your essay. If you have questions about the writing process, refer to Using the Writing Process on page 232.

- Assemble and review the work you did for all the writing exercises in this unit: 1) a list of your favorite poems from this book and the reasons you selected them; 2) a matching game involving five poems from this book and their themes; 3) an analysis of the words, details, and images that convey a speaker's tone in one poem; 4) a listing of the elements you would concentrate on in your analysis of a poem.
- In Writing on Your Own 3 you chose one poem to concentrate on. Now you will write an essay to evaluate that poem. If you wish to switch to a different poem, do so now. As you did for the first poem, jot down notes about the poem's poetic elements.
- Using your notes to guide you, write your first draft. Begin with a statement of the opinion you intend to support in your essay. Next, to help people who have not read the poem, provide a short summary or description of the poem. Then explain the strengths or weaknesses of the poem, providing supporting evidence for each of your opinions. Conclude with a general statement about why you like or dislike the poem.
- Proofread your essay for spelling, grammar, punctuation, and capitalization errors. Then make a clean copy of your essay. If any of your classmates have written about the same poem, trade essays and compare your opinions. Then save your essay in your writing portfolio.

USING THE WRITING PROCESS

This reference section explains the major steps in the writing process. It will help you complete the writing exercises in this book. Read the information carefully so you can understand the process thoroughly. Whenever you need a quick review of important things to think about when you write, refer to the handy checklist on page 238.

Most tasks worth doing have several steps. For example, houses can be built only after the builder follows a number of complicated, logical steps. Moviemakers must go through a series of steps before releasing a film. Even a task as simple as making a peanut butter and jelly sandwich requires that the sandwich maker perform specific steps in order. So it should be no surprise that anyone who wants to write a good story, play, poem, report, or article must follow certain steps too. Taken together, the steps a writer follows are called the *writing process*. This writing process is divided into three main stages: prewriting, writing, and revising. Each stage is important for good writing.

STAGE 1: Prewriting

Prewriting consists of all the preparation you do before you put a single word down on paper. There are many decisions that you must make in order to make your writing as interesting, logical, and easy to read as possible. Here are the steps you should take before you begin to write:

1. **Decide on your audience.** Who will read your writing? Will your audience be your teacher? Will it be readers of the school newspaper? Or will your audience be family or friends? Your writing will change, depending on who you think your audience will be.

2. **Decide on your purpose.** Why are you writing? Do you want to teach your audience something? Do you want to entertain

them? Do you want to change someone's mind about an issue? Think about your purpose before you begin to write.

3. **Think about possible topics.** What are some topics that interest you? Make a list of topics that you are familiar with and might like to write about. Make another list of topics that interest you and that you want to learn about.

   One technique that helps some writers at this stage is *brainstorming.* When you brainstorm, you let your mind wander freely. Without judging your ideas first, scribble them down as they come to you—even if they seem silly or farfetched. Good ideas often develop from unusual thoughts.

   If you're having trouble coming up with ideas by yourself, brainstorm with a partner or a group of classmates. Jot down everyone's ideas as they say them. Brainstorm-ing alone or with others should give you a long list of possible writing top-ics.

4. **Choose and narrow your topic.** Once you have chosen a topic, you will probably find that it is impossible to cover every aspect of it in one piece of writing. Say, for example, you have chosen to write about the possibility of life on other planets. In a single piece of writing, you could not possibly include everything that has been researched about extrater-restrial life. Therefore you must choose one or two aspects to focus on, such as alleged sightings in the United States or worldwide organizations that study extraterrestrial life. Otherwise you might overload your writing with too many ideas. Concentrate on telling about a few things thoroughly and well.

5. **Research your topic.** You probably have had experience using an encyclopedia, the library, or the Internet to look up infor-mation for factual reports. But even when you write fictional stories, you often need to do some research. In a story set during the Civil War, for example, your characters wouldn't use pocket cameras or wear suits of armor. In order to make

your story as accurate and believable as possible, you would have to research how Americans lived and dressed during the years of the Civil War.

To conduct your research, you may want to use books, magazines, newspapers, reference works, or electronic sources, such as the Internet. Some topics may require you to interview knowledgeable people. For realistic stories set in the present time, you may find that the best research is simple observation of everyday life. Thorough research will help ensure that your facts and details are accurate.

6. **Organize your research.** Now you have the facts, ideas, and details you need to write. How will you arrange them? Which order will you choose? No matter what you are writing, it is always helpful to begin with a written plan. If you are writing a story, you probably will tell it in time order. Make a list of the major story events, arranged from first to last.

Arranging details in time order is not the only way to organize information, however. Some writers start by making *lists* (informal outlines) of the facts and ideas they have gathered. Then they rearrange the items on their lists until they have the order that will work well in their writing.

Other writers make formal *outlines,* designating the most important ideas with roman numerals (I, II, III, IV, and so on) and related details with letters and numerals (A, B, C; 1, 2, 3; a, b, c; and so on). An outline is a more formal version of a list, and like the items in a list, the items in an outline can be rearranged until you decide on a logical order. Both outlines and lists help you organize and group your ideas.

Mapping or *clustering* is another helpful technique used by many writers. With this method, you write a main idea in the center of a cluster and then surround it with facts and ideas connected to that idea. Following is an example of a cluster map:

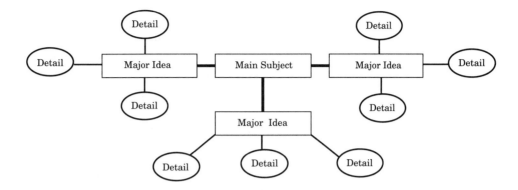

STAGE 2: Writing

1. **Get started.** Begin your writing with an introductory sentence or paragraph. A good introduction can become a guide for the rest of your piece. For ideas on good opening sentences, take a look at some of your favorite stories or magazine articles.

   Your introduction should give your audience a hint about what is coming next. If you are writing a story, your introduction should set the tone and mood. It should reveal the narrator's point of view; and it may introduce the main characters, the setting, and your purpose for writing. Do the best you can with your introduction, but remember that if you wish to, you can always change it later.

2. **Keep writing.** Get your thoughts down as quickly as possible, referring to your prewriting notes to keep you on track. Later, when you are done with this *rough draft,* you will have a chance to revise and polish your work to make it as clear and accurate as possible. For right now, however, don't stop for spelling, grammar, or exact wording problems. Come as close as you can to what you want to say, but don't let yourself get bogged down in details.

STAGE 3: Revising

Now you're ready to revise your work. Careful revision includes editing and reorganizing that can make a big difference in the final product. You may wish to get feedback from your classmates or your teacher about how to revise your work.

1. **Revise and edit your work.** When you are revising and editing, ask yourself these questions:
   - Did I follow my prewriting plan? Reread your entire first draft. Compare it to your original plan. Did you skip anything important? If you added an idea, did it work logically with the rest of your plan? Even if you decide that your prewriting plan is no longer what you want, it may include ideas you don't want to lose.
   - Is my writing clear and logical? Does one idea follow the other in a sensible order? Do you want to change the order or add ideas to make the organization clearer?
   - Is my language clear and interesting? Have you chosen exact verbs, nouns, and adjectives? For example, have you used forms of the verb *to be (is, are, being, become)* more often than you should? If so, replace them or change your sentence to make them unnecessary. Include precise action words such as *raced, hiked, zoomed,* and *hurried* in place of the overused verb *went.* Instead of using vague nouns such as *water* and *green,* choose exact ones such as *cascade* or *pond* and *lime.* Replace common adjectives such as *beautiful* and *nice* with precise ones such as *elegant, gorgeous,* and *lovely.*
   - Is my writing clear and to the point? Take out words that repeat the same ideas. For example, don't use both *liberty* and *freedom.* These words are synonyms. Choose one word or the other.

2. **Proofread for errors in spelling, grammar, capitalization, and punctuation.** Anyone reading your writing will notice such errors immediately. These errors can confuse your readers or make them lose interest in what they are reading.

If you are in doubt about the spelling of a word, look it up or ask someone for help. If you are unsure about your grammar, read your writing aloud and listen carefully. Does anything sound wrong? Check with a friend or classmate if you need a second opinion—or refer to a grammar handbook.

Make sure every group of words is a complete sentence. Are any of your sentences run-ons? Do proper nouns begin with capital letters? Is the first word of every sentence capitalized? Do all your sentences have the correct end marks? Should you add any other punctuation to your writing to make your ideas even clearer? If your writing includes dialogue, have you used quotation marks correctly?

3. **Make a clean final draft to share.** After you are satisfied with your writing, it is time to share it with your audience. If you are lucky enough to be composing on a computer, you can print out a final copy easily, after running a spell-check. If you are writing your final draft by hand, make sure your handwriting is clear and easy to read. Leave margins on either side of the page. You may want to skip every other line. Make your writing look inviting to your readers. After all, you put a lot of work into this piece. It's important that someone read and enjoy it.

A WRITING CHECKLIST

Ask yourself these questions before beginning a writing assignment:

- Have I chosen a topic that is both interesting and manageable? Should I narrow it so I can cover it in the space that I have?
- Do I have a clear prewriting plan?
- What should I do to gather my facts and ideas? read? interview? observe?
- How will I organize my ideas? In a list? an outline? a cluster map?
- Do I have an opening sentence or paragraph that will pull my readers in?
- Do I need to add more information? switch the order of paragraphs? take out unnecessary information?

Ask yourself these questions after completing a writing assignment:

- Did I use my prewriting plan?
- Is the organization of my writing clear? Should I move, add, or delete any paragraphs or sentences to make the ideas flow more logically?
- Do all the sentences in one paragraph relate to one idea?
- Have I used active, precise words? Is my language interesting? Do the words say what I mean?
- Are all the words spelled correctly?
- Have I used correct grammar, capitalization, punctuation, and formatting?
- Is my final draft legible, clean, and attractive?

GLOSSARY OF LITERARY TERMS

This glossary includes definitions for important literary terms that are introduced in this book. Boldfaced words within the definitions are other terms that appear in the glossary.

alliteration   the repetition of the same sounds within words that are close together. These sounds are usually consonant sounds that occur at the beginnings of words, but they also can occur within words.

anapest   metrical pattern in which two unstressed syllables come between stressed syllables and the stressed syllable regularly comes second ($\cup \cup /$).

apostrophe   the technique of addressing a thing or an absent person.

assonance   the repetition of vowel sounds within words.

audience   the particular person or group that a writer is addressing.

author's purpose   the reason an author writes. Four common author's purposes are to entertain, to inform, to persuade, and to express feelings or opinions.

blank verse   an unrhymed poem written in iambic pentameter.

character   a person, animal, or object that carries out the action of a poem.

cliché   an overused phrase or expression.

concrete language   words and phrases that describe things that readers can experience with their senses. *See* **image** and **sensory detail**.

concrete poem   a poem whose shape resembles the object it describes. This shape helps contribute to the meaning of the poem. *See* **iconograph**.

connotation   the emotion that a word arouses or the meaning it suggests beyond its **denotation**, or dictionary meaning.

239

consonance   a technique in which the consonant sounds at the ends of stressed syllables stay the same but the vowel sounds preceding them change, as in *pitter/patter* and *break/stick*.

couplet   a pair of lines that rhyme.

dactyl   metrical pattern in which two unstressed syllables come between stressed syllables and the stressed syllable regularly comes first ($/ \cup \cup$).

denotation   the literal, dictionary meaning of a word.

dialect   a version of a language spoken in one place or time, by one group of people.

dialogue   a conversation between two characters.

dramatic monologue   a poem with a single speaker who is engaged in a dramatic situation.

end rhyme   rhyme that occurs at the ends of lines of poetry.

extended metaphor   a special kind of metaphor that involves the entire poem. The individual metaphors within the poem contribute directly to the main metaphor. *See* **figure of speech, figurative language, metaphor,** and **implied metaphor.**

feminine rhyme   rhyming words that consist of a stressed syllable followed by one or more unstressed syllables, as in *neighbor* and *labor*. Feminine rhymes also can be made from two or more words together, as in *limit* and *dim it*.

figurative language   words and phrases used in such a way as to suggest something more than just their usual dictionary meanings. *See* **figure of speech.**

figure of speech   a word or phrase that suggests meanings other than the usual dictionary meaning. Most figures of speech involve comparisons. Some figures of speech are simile, metaphor, hyperbole, and personification.

first-person point of view   the vantage point, or perspective, in which the speaker is the person or character telling the story. When relating experiences from a first-person point of view, the speaker uses words such as *I, me,* and *we*. *See* **point of view** and **third-person point of view.**

foot   the unit in which meter is measured. A foot consists of one stressed syllable and one or more unstressed syllables. The number of feet in a line of poetry equals the number of stressed syllables. *See* **scanning** and **stress.**

free verse   poetry that does not have fixed rhythm, rhyme, meter, or line length. A poet using free verse is free to change patterns or to use no pattern at all.

haiku   a 3-line poem with 17 syllables. The first and third lines have 5 syllables each, and the second line has 7 syllables. The haiku, created first in Japan, expresses an experience by presenting one striking image.

hyperbole   a figure of speech that exaggerates the truth to emphasize an idea or feeling. *See* **figurative language.**

iamb   a metrical pattern consisting of one stressed and one unstressed syllable in which the unstressed syllable regularly comes first ($\cup$ /). *See* **meter** and **iambic pentameter.**

iambic pentameter   a line of poetry that contains five iambic feet. In English poetry iambic pentameter is used more often than any other meter.

iconograph   a poem that is written in the shape of the object it describes. *See* **concrete poem.**

image   a mental picture created with words or phrases. Images can appeal to any of the senses—sight, hearing, taste, smell, and touch. Some images appeal to more than one sense.

imagery   all the images that are created in a poem. *See* **image**.

implied metaphor   a kind of metaphor, also called *implicit metaphor*, in which one of the things being compared is not directly stated but is suggested by the context. "The shoppers swarmed into the store as soon as the doors opened" is an example of an implied metaphor in which the shoppers are indirectly compared to bees by the use of the word *swarmed*. *See* **figure of speech, figurative language, extended metaphor,** and **implied metaphor.**

internal rhyme   a rhyme that occurs when a word within a line rhymes with another word in the same line.

irony   the contrast between what is said and what is really meant or between what happens and what was expected to happen.

limerick   a short, humorous poem with five lines. Lines one, two, and five have three metric feet and lines three and four have two feet. The rhyme scheme is *aabba*.

lyric poem   a poem that has a single speaker and expresses a deeply felt thought or emotion. Lyric poems have a musical quality. Often in a lyric poem, the speaker does not have a specific audience, but instead is addressing himself or herself.

masculine rhyme   rhyming words with one syllable or one stressed syllable, as in *road* and *hoed* or *around* and *ground*.

metaphor   a figure of speech in which one thing is spoken about as if it were another, unlike thing. A metaphor helps readers *see* the similarities between these two things. *See* **figurative language, extended metaphor,** and **implied metaphor.**

meter   the regular rhythmic pattern of stressed and unstressed syllables in a line of poetry. Meter is counted in feet. The most common meter in English poetry is iambic pentameter. *See* **foot** and **stress.**

monologue   a poem in which only one speaker talks. *See* **dramatic monologue.**

mood   the general feeling or atmosphere created in a poem.

narrative poem   a poem that tells a story.

narrator   the speaker who tells the story in a narrative poem.

near-rhyme   a sound technique in which words with matching consonant sounds (**consonance**) or matching vowel sounds (**assonance**) are substituted for true rhymes, as in these word pairs: *wind/end* and *boat/hope*.

onomatopoeia   the use of words whose sounds imitate or suggest their meanings. Examples: *crash*, *buzz*, and *hiss*.

pentameter   a five-foot line. *See* **foot** and **meter**.

persona   the character who speaks in a poem. The poet speaks to the reader using that character's voice. *See* **speaker**.

personification   a figure of speech in which an animal, an object, or an idea is given human qualities. *See* **figurative language**.

point of view   vantage point from which a poem is written or a story is told. In a piece of literature written from a first-person point of view, the speaker uses words such as *I*, *me*, and *we*. In a piece written from the third-person point of view, the speaker uses the words *he*, *she*, and *they*.

prose   the ordinary form of written or spoken language, without any rhyme or regular rhythm. Short stories, novels, and essays are written in prose.

quatrain   a four-line stanza in a poem.

refrain   one or more lines that are repeated in a poem or a song.

repetition   the use of a sound, word, phrase, line, or **stanza** two or more times in a poem. *See* **refrain**.

rhyme   the repetition of ending sounds in two or more words. *See* **end rhyme, near-rhyme, masculine rhyme,** and **feminine rhyme**.

rhyme scheme   the pattern of end rhyme in a poem. The rhyme scheme can be determined if words at the ends of two or more lines rhyme. The rhyme scheme is shown by assigning a different letter of the alphabet to each line-end sound in a stanza. Lines that rhyme are given the same letter. For example, if the first and third lines rhyme and the second and fourth lines rhyme, the rhyme scheme is *abab*.

rhythm   the pattern of stressed and unstressed syllables in a poem. *See* **stress**.

scanning   counting the feet, or number and arrangement of stressed and unstressed syllables in a line, to determine the meter. *See* **foot** and **stress**.

sensory detail   words or phrases that describe the way things look, sound, taste, smell, or feel. Many sensory details together can create a **sensory image.**

sensory image   *See* **image**.

setting   the time or place of the action in a poem or a story.

simile   a figure of speech that compares two unlike things, using the word *like*, *as*, *appear*, or *seem*. *See* **figurative language**.

sonnet   a fourteen-line poem with a fixed pattern of rhythm and meter that follows one of several rhyme schemes. A Shakespearean sonnet has four parts—three quatrains and a couplet at the end. Its rhyme scheme is *abab cdcd efef gg*.

speaker   the voice that speaks in a poem. The speaker may or may not be the poet. Often the poet assumes a persona, or alternate identity. *See* **narrator**.

stanza   a group of lines in a poem. Each stanza in a rhyming poem often has the same **rhyme scheme.** *See* **quatrain**.

stress   the emphasis given to a word or syllable. A strongly stressed syllable is marked with a straight line (/) and an unstressed syllable is marked with a curved line (∪), as in this example:

/ ∪   / ∪ /∪ /

Twinkle, twinkle, little star

structure   the overall design of a work. Structure refers to the way a poet arranges words, lines, and ideas to produce a particular effect.

symbol   a person, place, or thing that stands for something else.

tercet   three lines that may or may not contain **end rhyme.**

theme   the insight or message that an author conveys in a piece of writing.

third-person point of view   the point of view, or perspective, in which the speaker stands outside the action and tells the story using words such as *he, she,* and *they. See* **first-person point of view** and **point of view.**

tone   a writer's attitude toward his or her subject, audience, or self.

trochee   a metrical pattern consisting of one stressed and one unstressed syllable in which the stressed syllable regularly comes first (/ ∪).

verse paragraph   a group of lines in a poem that forms a unit similar to that of a prose paragraph. A verse paragraph's length varies according to the requirements of the thought that is being expressed.

villanelle   a 19-line poem composed of five tercets and an ending quatrain. The first and third lines of the first tercet are repeated alternately as the third line of the other tercets and as the third and fourth lines of the quatrain. The best-known villanelle is "Do Not Go Gentle into That Good Night" by Dylan Thomas.

(continued from page iv)

Stanton, Maura. "Childhood" by Maura Stanton. Reprinted from *Maura Stanton: Cries of Swimmers* by permission of Carnegie Mellon Univesity Press © 1984 by Maura Stanton.

Stephens, James. "Check" from *Collected Poems* by James Stephens. Copyright 1915 by Macmillan Publishing Co., Inc., renewed 1943 by James Stephens. Reprinted by permission of The Society of Authors as the Literary Representative of the Estate of James Stephens.

Swenson, May. "Water Picture" is reprinted with permission of Simon & Schuster Books for Young Readers, an imprint of Simon & Schuster Children's Publishing Division from *The Complete Poems To Solve* by May Swenson. Copyright © 1966 May Swenson. (First appeared in *The New Yorker*).

Swenson, May. "Unconscious Came a Beauty" is reprinted with the permission of Simon & Schuster Books for Young Readers, an imprint of Simon & Schuster Children's Publishing Division from *The Complete Poems To Solve* by May Swenson. Copyright © 1993 The Literary Estate of May Swenson.

Teasdale, Sara. "Hide and Seek" is reprinted with the permission of Simon & Schuster from *Mirror of the Heart: Poems of Sara Teasdale* edited by William Drake. Copyright © 1984 by The Morgan Guaranty Trust Company of New York. From the Collection of American Literature, the Beinecke Rarebook and Manuscript Library, Yale University.

Teasdale, Sara. "The Kiss" is reprinted with the permission of Simon & Schuster from *The Collected Poems of Sara Teasdale* by Sara Teasdale. Copyright © 1937 by Macmillan Publishing Company; copyright renewed 1965.

Walker, Alice. "Medicine" from *Once*, copyright © 1968 and renewed 1996 by Alice Walker, reprinted by permission of Harcourt Brace & Company.

Walker, Margaret. "Molly Means" by Margaret Walker Alexander in *This Is My Century*. Athens, Georgia: Georgia State Press, 1989. Reprinted by permission of the author.

Welch, James. "The Man from Washington" is reprinted by permission of James Welch from *Riding the Earthboy 40: Poems, 1971*. Copyright 1971 by James Welch. All rights reserved.

West, Peter. "It's Hot in the City," from *Voices of Literature Book 1*, compiled by Dr. Marshall McLuhan and Dr. Richard J. Schoeck, 1964.

Weston, Mildred. "Central Park Tourney," *The New Yorker* Magazine, May 9, 1953. Reprinted by permission; © 1953 *The New Yorker* Magazine, Inc. All rights reserved.